# New Military Museums

John Zukowsky

# New Military Museums

Edition Axel Menges

Underwritten exclusively by the Chicago Marine Heritage Society and its Chairman Capt. Dave Truitt


ISBN 978-3-86905-015-7



Printing and binding: Graspo CZ, a.s., Zlín, Czech Republic

Editing: Nora Krehl-von Mühlendahl
Design: Axel Menges

## Contents

## New military museums: honoring service and sacrifice

Art museums are often considered to be the epitome of museum architecture. I should know, I worked at one for more than two and a half decades in the last quarter of the twentieth century. All you have to do is browse the architecture and design magazines over that time period to see that this is true. From the 1970s through the first decade of the twenty-first century, the whole world witnessed a host of them being constructed – many of them by »A-list« architects. In the United States, these include the National Gallery of Art addition designed by I.M. Pei and the Metropolitan Museum's new Sackler Wing to house the Temple of Dendur by Roche and Dinkeloo, both opening 1978. Newer ones include Renzo Piano's Modern Wing of the Art Institute of Chicago (2009) and his Whitney Museum of American Art (2015), along with Norman Foster's Art of the Americas Wing at the Museum of Fine Arts in Boston (2010), and more recently the Broad Museum (2015) by Diller, Scofidio and Renfro.

This phenomenon was not only seen within America's borders. Perhaps the most famous examples are Parisian, such as the Centre George Pompidou (1977) by Piano and Rogers, the Musée d'Orsay (1986) by Gae Aulenti, and the Grand Louvre (1989) by I.M. Pei. Frank Gehry's Guggenheim Bilbao (1997) in Spain brought this to another level. The latter inspired a two-decade long competitive building boom by »star architects« designing major art museums that recently witnessed the completion of Jean Nouvel's Louvre Abu Dhabi (2017) in the United Arab Emirates. When you think about it, high profile architects have almost always been the ones to build major art museums even before then, especially in the International Modernist era after World War II (1939–45). Buildings such as Frank Lloyd Wright's Guggenheim Museum in New York (1959), Ludwig Mies van der Rohe's Neue Nationalgalerie in Berlin (1968), and Louis Kahn's Kimbell Art Museum (1971) in Fort Worth are in just about every architectural survey. This doesn't mean that history or science museums have been completely ignored over those decades. Examples that come to my mind are the Holocaust Memorial Museum (1993) in Washington, D.C., by James Ingo Freed of I.M. Pei (illus. 1) with its dramatic exhibitions by Ralph Appelbaum, the I.M. Pei addition to the Zeughaus in Berlin (2006) to create the Deutsches Historisches Museum in Berlin, the Cité des Sciences et de l'Industrie (2006) in Paris by Adrien Fainsilber, and David Adjaye's National Museum of African American History and Culture (2016) in Washington, D.C., also with Appelbaum-designed installations.

Even though you would find some science centers or history museums touted within this sequence, the art museum most certainly received the lion's share of magazine publicity in terms of recognizing professionalism of presentation. This also goes beyond big-budget major facilities cited above to somewhat smaller ones that have received acclaim in their own time, from Philip Johnson's Munson-Williams-Proctor Arts Institute (1960) in Utica, New York, to the Glass Pavilion of the Toledo Museum of Art (2006) in Ohio by Kazuyo Sejima and Ryue Nishizawa, and Shigeru Ban's Aspen Art Museum (2014) in Colorado.

By comparison, when we think of military museums, we often think of a stereotype of antiquated buildings and their exhibit installations as staid or amateurish. Military museums, however, have had a design renaissance since the 1990s. Perhaps this relates to a greater appreciation of military service and sacrifice since the successful coalition in the Gulf War of 1991. This is so not only in the United States but also throughout the world, and especially in the United Kingdom, in part, because of lottery support of museums. This book intends to visually survey examples from the early 1990s through the present in terms of this newfound appreciation, especially as regards new architecture and exhibition design. I believe it is the first such volume to do so. Although not a definitive survey, it brings together museums from across the globe, done over the past twenty-five years. It is my hope that readers will view newer military museums as significant as other museum types in terms of the sophistication of their buildings and installations. Before we embark on this pictorial survey, it would be good to review some historic architectural examples that commemorate the military, either in free-standing sculptural memorials or actual buildings. This will not be a comprehensive survey of war memorials nor like museums, yet the ones discussed in this introduction will help to provide a context for understanding those museum buildings being done today.

### The war memorial, past and present

A number of military museums use words such as commemorate, honor, inspire and educate within their mission statements and taglines. Their exhibits and missions are often both commemorative, as well as memorializing. War memorials themselves have a prolific past that dates back millennia, with examples in Egyptian obelisks, and Roman triumphal arches and victory columns. Specific monuments such as the Arch of Titus c. 81CE and Trajan's Column of 113 CE are directly associated with Imperial military victories. These are illustrated with narratives of conquest, depicted in relief sculptures on those triumphal forms. The triumphal arch, victory column, and even variations on the obelisk, are forms long associated with historicist war memorials in the nineteenth and twentieth centuries. They can be seen across the globe commemorating various wars, leaders, and their combatants. Some of these are obvious to tourists. They include: the Bunker Hill Battle Monument (1843) in Boston, Massachusetts, an obelisk 221 feet (67.4m) high designed by Solomon Willard; the 169 feet (51.5 m) high Nelson Column (1843) in London's Trafalgar Square, designed by William Railton and others, and dedicated to Admiral Horatio Nelson's 1805 victory; the 219 feet (67 m) high Siegessäule or Victory Column in Berlin (1873) by Heinrich Strack, with the gilt bronze statue of *Victoria* by Friedrich Drake, all commemorating Otto von Bismarck's wars to unify Germany; and the 164 feet (50 m) high Arc de Triomphe (1836) at the Champs-Élysées in Paris, designed by Jean-François-Thérèse Chalgrin in 1806 to commemorate Napoleon's victory over Russia and Austria at Austerlitz.

Variations on these major landmarks can be found across the globe. Perhaps the largest may

1. The United States Holocaust Memorial Museum, Washington, D.C., 1993. Photo: Carol M. Highsmith Archive, Library of Congress, Prints and Photographs Division.
2. Thiepval Memorial, Thiepval, France, 1932. Photo: shutterstock.com.
3. Kriegerdenkmal im Hofgarten, Munich, 1924. Photo: shutterstock.com.
4. Indiana War Memorial Museum, Indianapolis, 1933. Photo: Carol M. Highsmith Archive, Library of Congress, Prints and Photographs Division.
5. Soldier Field, Chicago, 2003. Photo: shutterstock.com.

be ones that commemorate World War I (1914 to 1918). This proverbial »war to end all wars« experienced more than 18 million civilians and military personnel dead and 23 million wounded. This was a staggering number that was more than four to five times the deaths during the Napoleonic Wars a century earlier. World War I memorials include large and small-scale variants of columns, obelisks, and triumphal arches as well as more Modernist plinths and slabs. They include the powerful Thiepval Memorial (1932), a monumentally arched, 140 feet (43 m) high stone and brick monument. It was created by Sir Edwin Lutyens to commemorate more than 72,000 missing British and South African troops during the Battle of the Somme in 1916 (illus. 2). Others were either subject referenced or more abstract, the latter influenced by the increasing simplicity of Modernist design in the 1920s. The stylized ship-like prow of the 233 feet (71 m) high Marine-Ehrenmal or Naval Memorial (1936) in Laboe near Kiel, by Gustav August Munzer, is dedicated to all navy personnel who died in wars. Modernist planar ones include the simple slabs of the Kriegerdenkmal (1924) in Munich's Hofgarten by Thomas Wechs and Eberhard Finsterwalder or the Ehrenmal (1931) stele in Hamburg's Rathausmarkt by Klaus Hoffmann and Ernst Barlach. The Munich example (illus. 3) reminds us of the tension between Modernist and realist memorial representations. Here the sculpted fallen German soldier is seen akin to a medieval knight's tomb within a rectilinear masonry chapel.

Perhaps because of the conflict's scale and the desire to create numerous memorials of various size, the period during those interwar years witnessed what may be the start of buildings being dedicated as memorials to the war. For instance, Soldier Field (illus. 5) in Chicago was originally built as the Municipal Grant Park Stadium (1924) by architects Holabird and Roche, though it was dedicated two years later during the Army–Navy football game to commemorate Chicago's war dead. A 2003 renovation involved restoration of the stadium's massive Doric arcade, creation of a Medal of Honor section, installation of a 250 feet (76.2 m) long memorial wall, and restoration and installation of a famed Doughboy statue by sculptor E.M. Viquesney. Other useful memorial buildings were constructed at this time in America, including what are early examples of military memorial museums in a more modern sense of the word, despite being traditional in appearance.

One is the Indiana War Memorial Plaza and Indiana War Memorial Museum. It was begun 1919 and dedicated 1933 even before completion, designed by Cleveland architects Walker and Weeks with New York sculptor Henry Hering (illus. 4). This landscaped and planned 24 acres (9.7 ha) space in Indianapolis contains the museum housed within a massive building whose design is based on the legendary Mausoleum at Halicarnassus (ca. 350 BCE), one of the great wonders of the ancient world. Another early example is the severely Classicist Soldiers' Memorial Military Museum (1936) in St. Louis, Missouri, built by local architects Mauran, Russell & Crowell to showcase war trophies from the Great War. In some ways those two examples in Indianapolis and St. Louis were an extension of the Grand Army of the Republic/GAR halls of an earlier generation. The GAR was founded 1866 as an association of Civil War (1861–65) veterans of the Union armed forces. In the last decade of the nineteenth century they had 490,000 members.

One such GAR meeting hall was within the 1897 Chicago Public Library by Shepley, Rutan and Coolidge. There, Civil War memorabilia and artifacts were displayed as war trophies. Roman trophy-relief sculptures still adorn entry arches to the GAR hall, now a room for changing art exhibitions which is in what is currently the Chicago Cul-

tural Center. The Pittsburgh Soldiers and Sailors Memorial Hall and Museum by Henry Hornbostel (1910) was an outgrowth of the GAR there. Its museum collection focused early on the Civil War and Battle of Gettysburg, but also continues with artifacts through today. Its Classicist building design prefigures the Indianapolis memorial in some ways. Those buildings from the first decades of the twentieth century were paralleled in this museum function by the Liberty Memorial (1926), later National World War I Memorial and Museum, in Kansas City (see p. 40).

The American memorial museums above were followed by the Australian War Memorial (1941) in Canberra, that nation's capital (illus. 6). It houses the domed Hall of Memory with the Australian tomb of the unknown soldier on the upper level, with museum exhibits, and a research center at the ground and lower levels. It was the brainchild of Australia's official historian of World War I Charles Bean and long-time director Major John Treloar. A 1927 competition produced no clear winner but Sydney competitors Emil Sodersten and John Crust partnered together here to prepare the design. Today, the museum features an active program of exhibitions, several of which were created by Australian exhibit designers Freeman Ryan Design. In all, it seems that what we know as a modern military museum has antecedents created mostly after World War I, in part, because they also served as war memorials.

As with the tension between abstract and Classicist or realistic memorial representations, which continued into the future, the so-called functional or living memorial also saw an expansion of use after the next world conflict. World War II (1939 to 1945) was a global one that witnessed the death of more than 60 million. We shall examine some of those later within this discussion. For our purposes now, sculptural freestanding memorials continued to be built to honor the dead for that and several wars throughout the twentieth century. They included traditional architectural and sculptural forms as well as new abstract, dynamic shapes that also have specific military references. Of realistic traditional sculptures, perhaps the most internationally recognizable are two that also reflect the postwar Cold War between west and east – the United States and its allies, and the Soviet Union and its Warsaw Pact. The heroic figures of Felix de Weldon's *Marine Corps Memorial* (1954) outside Washington, D.C., achieved iconic status because of its relationship with the famed 1945 photo of the Iwo Jima flag raising by Joe Rosenthal. The colossal monument titled *The Motherland Calls* (1967) outside Volgograd, formerly Stalingrad, was created by sculptor Yevgeny Vuchetich and engineer Nikolai Nikitin. When built, it was the largest sculpture in the world at 279 feet (85 m) high. The architecture below houses a tomb for two heroes of the Battle of Stalingrad, Marshall Vasily Ivanovich Chuikov and Red Army sniper Vasily Zaytsev, the latter memorialized in the feature film *Enemy at the Gates* (2001).

Other memorials of the same era include military hardware almost as an extension of exhibiting the war trophy. Only now it is the trophy of the victor, not the vanquished – as in the Soviet War memorial in Berlin's Tiergarten (1945) by architect Mikhail Gorvits and sculptors Vladimir Tsigal and Lev Kerbel. Stylized Classicist architecture built from masonry of the Reichskanzlei and a sculpted soldier are flanked by artillery pieces and T-34/76 tanks on pedestals (illus. 7). The monument commemorates and memorializes the 2,000 Soviet soldiers who died and were buried here in the liberation of Berlin during World War II. It is joined by other Soviet war memorials in the city commemorating the 80,000 soldiers who died here in that struggle. Perhaps the most famous is the large memorial in Berlin's Treptower Park (1949), also built with stones from the Reichskanzlei as a memorial to the 7,000 Russian soldiers buried there.

This reliance on traditional figural sculptures or references to actual wartime artifacts, especially for military memorials, continues to reappear even after the public has been exposed to abstract sculptural and architectural forms over several decades. Such abstract geometric forms are the basis of memorials such as Egypt's concrete *Tomb of the Unknown Soldier* (1975), 120 feet (36.6 m) high, by artist Sami Rafi. It commemorates those who died in the 1973 October War. It also houses the tomb of President Anwar Sadat who commissioned the memorial in 1974 (illus. 8). The 246 feet (75 m) long angular black granite walls of the *Vietnam Veterans Memorial* (1982) in Washington, D.C., designed by Maya Lin slash into the landscape, visually symbolizing that war as a wound in the nation (illus. 9). Yet both of those monuments also recall specific associations from the past despite their seemingly abstract forms: the former of the great pyramids of Egypt, and the latter, the simple private first-class stripe of an American infantry soldier. One of the newer nonrepresentational ones is the International Bomber Command Centre (2015) in Lincoln, England (illus. 10) designed by Stephen Palmer of Place Architecture. The 102 feet (31 m) high monument looks quite abstract but it also references the size and shape of Avro Lancaster bomber wings from World War II. The grounds include a 2018 visitor center as one would find today on a historic battlefield, with interpretive interactive exhibitions designed by Redman Design. In a way, the Bomber Command spire prompts us to cite the various abstract compositions of steel pieces from the ruined World Trade Center destroyed in the terrorist attacks of September 11, 2001. These are used in countless 911 memorials at varying scales across the United States and beyond.

Despite this international acceptance of artistic abstraction over the past six decades, others consider geometric forms still not enough to memorialize a war, tragic event, or heroic people. Witness the backlash to the Vietnam Veteran's Memorial which eventually led to figural sculptures being installed (1984) in the complex. The subsequent creation of the Korean War Veterans Memorial (1995) in Washington, D.C., coordinated by Cooper-Lecky Architects, with its nineteen realistic stainless-steel soldiers created by sculptor Frank Gaylord, or the retro-Classicist, granite World War II Memorial (illus. 11) won in 1997 competition by Austrian-American architect Friedrich St. Florian (dedicated 2004), all reinforce that conservatism when it comes to war memorials of this type.

6. Australian War Memorial, Canberra, 1941. Photo: shutterstock.com.
7. Soviet War Memorial, Tiergarten, Berlin, 1945. Photo: shutterstock.com.
8. Egyptian Tomb of the Unknown Soldier, Cairo, 1974. Photo: shutterstock.com.
9. Vietnam Veterans Memorial, Washington, D.C. Photo: Carol M. Highsmith's America, Library of Congress, Prints and Photographs Division.
10. Spire of the International Bomber Command Centre, Canwick Hill, Lincoln, England, 2018. Photo: Tim Burton, SH Structures.
11. World War II Memorial, Washington, D.C., 2004. Carol M. Highsmith's America, Library of Congress, Prints and Photographs Division.
12. Peace Museum, Hiroshima, 1955. Photo: shutterstock.com.

### World War II and the living memorial

We have already referenced some post-World War I examples when buildings serve as war memorials, including some memorial buildings that have museums within. After World War II, the trend intensified for functional memorials as veterans' organizations spearheaded efforts to support buildings that promoted peace and reconciliation. This happened in the United States in 1944 even before the end of the war, with the American Legion publishing plans and elevations by Tennessee architect Eli M. Tinsdale for local posts that could serve as community centers. Likewise, the American Commission for Living War Memorials also published, in 1944 and 1945, booklets of plans and photos in order to inspire communities to build parks, sports, and health facilities, appropriately labeled with memorial plaques. War memorial arenas and stadia followed across the country. Nations built memorials as athletic, religious reconciliatory, or informal educational facilities. These include a Modernist Canadian War Memorial Gymnasium from 1951 at the University of British Columbia, designed by Sharp, Thompson, Berwick and Pratt. Long recognized international examples related to peace and reconciliation include: the Peace Park and Museum in Hiroshima (1955) by Kenzo Tange; the Kaiser-Wilhelm-Gedächtniskirche in Berlin (1961) by Egon Eiermann; and Sir Basil Spence's Coventry Cathedral (1962). Tange's work in Hiroshima (illus. 12) serves as one of the early post World War II examples of a military-related museum, though in an indirect way, memorializing civilian victims rather than combatants. Its clean, Modernist design ushered in a new era of Japanese architecture, signaling to the world that Japan has joined the postwar western world in its embrace of Modernist design.

Modernist designs followed in other memorial buildings, and two deserve mention. The first is the Eero Saarinen-designed Milwaukee County War Memorial (1957) in Wisconsin. It functioned as a meeting space for veterans groups and the community, but also as the first home of the Milwaukee Art Museum before various expansions, including their 2001 building by Santiago Calatrava. Artist Edmund D. Lewandowski created the mosaic mural two years after the building's completion. The 1,800 square feet (167 sq. m) mosaic contains more than a million pieces which include date references to the American involvement in World War II and the Korean War. When installed, it was then the largest mosaic in the United States.

Even more important both as a monument and as a work of architecture is the U.S.S. *Arizona* Memorial at Pearl Harbor (1962) designed by Albert Preis (see p. 22). The memorial was built as a public-private partnership of more than $ 500,000, including donations of $ 64,000 from an Elvis Presley benefit concert. As part of the building requirements, Preis created an expressive bridge-like structure that could accommodate 200 people for a contemplative visit above the submerged battleship *Arizona.* The ship sunk on December 7, 1941 during the Japanese attack on Pearl Harbor that precipitated America's entry into the war. The memorial is a national one to all who died there that day. Its design is more an open-air chapel than bridge, being approached only through a naval launch. Beyond being a memorial visited by two million people each year, it is the centerpiece of what later became an open air military museum, with the nearby former battleship *Missouri* as well as the naval air station at Ford Island, now site of the Pacific Aviation Museum. Although a visitor center was constructed 1980 and then expanded 2010, it is a background building in design, compared to this memorial which raised the bar for military memorial design in the United States as well as, eventually, design of military museums. Its seaside location has required several concrete repair campaigns, the latest in 2018.

### The military museum: ancient origins and modern manifestations

Arguably, the military museum ultimately derives from display of war booty – war trophies of vanquished armies brought home by victors to celebrate their triumphs, often depicted within relief narratives in ancient monuments. But what was the first museum dedicated to the collection and display of such material? It is difficult to say. Museums in a conceptual way date back to the Greek word *mouseion,* or muses, though we really cannot determine what they looked like in antiquity, even in Plato's famed library and museum. In the seventeenth and eighteenth centuries they were more like cabinets of curiosities, and indeed some may have held military artifacts. Scholars credit regiments as having collections of battle standards and war trophies. One of the earliest of regimental museum collections was said to have been at the »Kaiser-Jäger-Regiment« in Austria from the early 1800s. Another early museum collection and permanent building was one within the Royal Arsenal in Woolwich, England – the Repository for Military Machines. Created after 1770, it showcased artillery pieces to the public in the Rotunda of 1820, designed by John Nash. The objects displayed there became the core of the Royal Artillery Museum nearby. After 2016 they were placed in storage as part of the planning for the Salisbury Plain Heritage Centre, designed by Purcell Architects and scheduled to open 2020. Nash's historic Rotunda, however, still remains but is not open to the public.

The Woolwich example is a good one as a precedent for a purpose built military museum, open to the public. Perhaps an even better one in terms of collection is the Royal Armouries in the Tower of London, the oldest continually operating museum of arms and armaments back to the 1680s. And in terms of the first national army museum, it is likely to be the French Army Museum or Musée de l'Armée. It was established officially in 1905 within the gigantic Hôtel national des Invalides in Paris, which also contains Napoleon's tomb. Both the London and Paris institutions have comprehensive collections that date back through the Middle Ages and also document artifacts up through today.

The first half of the twentieth century and particularly the interwar years saw the establishment of other military museums from Moscow to Madrid, many in buildings that were inherited rather than commissioned. The post-World War II era, however, was also important in establishing and re-purposing other buildings related to militaria, particularly on important military sites such as battlefields. These can serve a variety of functions, and at some historic battlefields, principally as interpretive centers for the public.

During 1942/43, German architect Friedrich Tamms designed anti-aircraft gun emplacements atop castle-like, concrete bomb shelters. They housed thousands during Allied bombing raids of Berlin, Hamburg, and Vienna. These and some smaller counterparts by others around Germany and occupied Europe sometimes proved too difficult to demolish in the postwar era. They were often adapted to other functions, from film and radio studios, to art galleries, and even restaurants and bars. These conversions continue today, one of the more notable being the Museumscenter Blåvand, now opened as the Tirpitz Museum, in Varde, Denmark (2017). It was designed by Bjarke Ingels, Jakob Lange, and David Zahle of BIG, with Tinker imagineers creating the visitor experience (illus. 13). The core of the new museum building is the unfinished ruin of the Tirpitz bunker, with the concrete and glass museum sliced into the earth. It now houses interactive exhibitions and media presentations about the site, before, during and after the war. In some ways this dramatic renewal bears comparison with the archaeological presentation of the Louvre's original castle walls when I.M. Pei created not only the Louvre Pyramid (1999) but also the underground mall that connects the museums wings and has services related to retail, food, and parking. As with that Parisian example, this dramatic redo is intended to make it a tourist attraction in Denmark.

When speaking of military sites, new interpretive centers were also built in relation to historic battlefields. As with museums they may incorporate artifacts within their displays but their focus is about interpreting the historic site that exists outside their doors, either through exhibits or media presentations. They also often include restaurants, cafes and retail stores for their public. A less well-known but important recent example is the Culloden Battlefield Visitor Center (2007) designed by Gareth Hoskins Architects with Ralph Appelbaum Associates creating the exhibitions (illus. 14). An earlier significant one existed in Richard Neutra's Gettysburg Visitor Center (1962) in Pennsylvania. The building was part of an initiative to create modern visitor centers at American national parks in the 1960s. After much debate and preservation controversy, it was demolished 2013 since its function as a visitor center was replaced at a nearby site by a contextual, historicist building, designed by Warehaus (2008/09). (Compare illus. 15, with p. 64.)

Perhaps the most amazing battlefield museum is the one in Volgograd, Russia, which commemorates one of the major turning points of World War II, the Battle of Stalingrad. The battle which lasted from August 23, 1942 through February 2, 1943 killed both Axis soldiers and Russians to a total of some 1.9 million causalities, decimating the entire city as well. The memorial museum built to commemorate this Russian victory found its conceptual origins even before the end of the battle, first opening in 1948. What exists today is a research center and museum of more than 3,500 artifacts and major dioramas along with a spectacular painted 360-degree panorama. This is the largest painting in Russia at 393x52 feet (120x16 m). That depiction of the battle is augmented by three-dimensional dioramas in the foreground. The museum and panorama rotunda (illus. 16) was the design work of architect Vadim Maslyaev, finished 1985. The complex also has a 1903 ruined mill in situ from the battle as well as a reproduction, installed 2013, of the Barmaley fountain of dancing children. This was memorialized in a famous 1942 photograph of Stalingrad's ruins taken by Emma-nuil Evzerikhin.

In some ways, interpretive centers at concentration camps and military cemeteries also are part of this tradition of battlefield museums and similar centers. One of the bolder designed ones is the Hinzert Museum and Document Centre (2005) at the former Hinzert Concentration Camp in Germany. Nikolaus Hirsch and Wolfgang Lorch created the angular structure from 3,000 welded corten-steel panels. Several contemporary centers also commemorate the Allied invasion of occupied France on D-Day, June 6, 1944. Two are discussed within this volume, the Canadian Juno Beach Centre (2003; see. p. 30) by Brian Chamberlain and the American Cemetery Visitor Center, Normandy (2007; see p. 52) by the Smith Group JJR and Gallagher & Associates.

Beyond interpretive centers at war-related sites, purpose-built major military museums saw a rise in the 1970s and 80s. Prominent ones include the National Army Museum in London (1971; see p. 104) by William Holford & Partners, and the National Army Museum (1978) in New Zealand. The latter is the Queen Elizabeth II Army Memorial Museum in Waiouru, New Zealand, built by the 2nd Field

13. Tirpitz Museum, Blåvand, Denmark, 2017. Photo: dpa picture alliance/Alamy Stock Photo.
14. Culloden Visitor Center, Inverness, Scotland, 2007. Photo: John Peter Photography/Alamy Stock Photo.
15. Gettysburg Battlefield Visitor Center, Gettysburg, Pennsylvania, 1962 (demolished). Photo: Library of Congress, Prints & Photographs Division, HABS PA-6709.
16. Volgograd State Panoramic Museum for the Battle of Stalingrad, 1985. Photo: shutterstock.com.
17. National Army Museum, Waiouru, New Zealand, 1978, with Centurion tank in the foreground. Photo: shutterstock.com.
18. Imperial War Museum, London. Photo: shutterstock.com.
19. Imperial War Museum, London. Lobby renovation, 1989. Photo: incamerastock/Alamy Stock Photo.
20. Stuart Light Tank in a Diorama on the Battle of Buna-Gona in World War II, Wisconsin Veterans Museum, Madison, Wisconsin. Photo: Daderot, Wikimedia.

Squadron of the Royal New Zealand Engineers (illus. 17). Both of those museums are constructed in what was then popular Brutalist concrete forms that project a fortress or barrack-like image to the visitor. Museums such as those were important in establishing the design credibility of such public military museums. One of the most important of these is the Imperial War Museum/IWM in London.

As with some of its international counterparts, it was founded 1917 as a World War I memorial museum. It has been housed in its present location within the former Bethlem Royal Hospital in London since 1936, its trademark dome being the 1846 work of Sydney Smirke. The fifteen-inch naval guns from the former World War I battleships HMS *Ramillies* and HMS *Resolution* were installed after 1967. They symbolically guard the entry (illus. 18) and visually rebrand the building's function. Over the next decades the Imperial War Museum became a leader of such institutions, expanding collections and sites to include the War Cabinet Rooms and heavy cruiser HMS *Belfast*, both in London, and an aviation collection at the former Royal Air Force field of Duxford in Cambridgeshire (see p. 18). The main campus, however, witnessed major expansions and renovations in 1986–89 by Arup (illus. 19) as well as most recently by Foster+Partners (see p. 80). The IWM's 1989 installation and gallery renovations, constructed through 1995, gave visitors an exciting glimpse into the future regarding immersive battle scenes, touch screen interactives and historically accurate flight simulator experiences that are commonplace in today's military museums. For the main lobby, Arup created a lightweight steel structure with a barrel vault atop where aircraft might be hung.

During subsequent years the museum hosted exhibits whose cutting-edge designs and themes helped broaden their audience, even in terms of architecture. Subjects ranged from the 1996 show »From the Bomb to the Beatles« on postwar Britain, designed by Sir Terrence Conran, to the 1997 American Air Museum at Duxford designed by Norman Foster (see p. 18), through the reconstruction of a 1940s house (2001–11) that was part of a television series, as well as the 2002 opening of the IWM North in Manchester, designed by Daniel Libeskind (see p. 26). The IWM was the pathfinder military museum in terms of examining the role of the military in relation to society. This is something that was subsequently taken up by other museums in their permanent installations, such as the Militärhistorisches Museum der Bundeswehr in Dresden (p. 72) and the National Army Museum in London (p. 104). The IWM's focus on visitor experience and customer service, expanded audiences, and the ability to offer a wide range of popular activities and exhibitions over all their facilities, brings them consistently to the forefront of military museums over the decades. Their sites are visited by more than 2.4 million people annually – certainly attendance on a par with many major museums elsewhere.

### Military museum exhibition design: beyond mannequins and dioramas

Unlike design collections within art museums that display chairs and cars on pedestals, keeping you at arm's reach from those precious artifacts, military museum exhibits today derive from both history and science museums, in their attitudes towards visitor interactions with machines. Visitors go to museums to learn the truth about history through original artifacts and stories about real people. This sometimes causes problems with the display of real artifacts compared with replicas and theatrical creations or stage sets, as well as intermingles the touch and do-not-touch experiences for museum goers. Understandably, this causes some confusion and can send mixed messages if museums are not cautious. In one instance, a visitor questioned me about a display that showed wooden constructions to represent concrete sidewalks, asking if the streets were made of wood, how come they didn't burn in the disaster depicted. Visitors often take stage sets and theatrical environments literally, as they do with mannequins and dioramas, perhaps because they are in museums, as opposed to seeing sets within a play or feature film. Although replica aircraft and military machines are sometimes used in museum displays, in contrast with focusing on original artifacts, we might also be reminded that replicas have long been used in military exhibits to give people a sense of scale and context. The same might be said of dioramas. So the situation is more grey than black and white when it comes to theatrical contexts within military museum displays.

I suppose these are three-dimensionalized representations of scenes formerly depicted centuries earlier in massive two-dimensional history paintings done in oil on canvas. In the United States, one of the most famous is by French artist Paul Dominique Phillipoteaux in his 1883, 360-degree painting of Pickett's Charge at the Battle of Gettysburg, 1863. It, as other such encyclopedic views, were displayed within cylindrical buildings called cycloramas, this one from 1883 being first shown in Chicago. Another painted in 1884 was displayed in Boston. That one is the only one to survive, being displayed for years at the Gettysburg visitor center up through today (see p. 64).

Along with some panoramic history paintings and cycloramic art, dioramas within museums were first used in the nineteenth century, though within a natural history context to show representations of animals in their habitat. The process of showing a snapshot scene within a frame, illuminated from within or behind, is related to early photography as well as paintings on translucent surfaces. Indeed, the word diorama is credited to photography pioneer Louis Daguerre. The tradition of creating scenes in three dimensions also relates to the long-time popularity of smaller scale miniatures. And the connection to model railroads, toy soldiers, and military hobbyists today is a natural one. When represented full size within military museums, some of these events are more successful than others, and mannequin features range from hyper-realistic to somewhat unconvincing. In whatever form, they often help provide the human connection to a historic event.

As hinted before, the full-size diorama of a military scene (illus. 20) is akin to what large scale history paintings were in the nineteenth century in their attempts to bring a historic event to life. With those theatrical sets today, a lot depends on budget regarding how realistic the scenography can

appear, as in the National Museum of the Marine Corps with life cast features in their mannequins. When the Art Institute of Chicago reinstalled their arms and armor collection in 2017, they even re-created knights jousting on mannequin horses by carefully replicating the forms of medieval war horses as based on their Lipizzaner descendants from a nearby farm. Whatever the reason, visitors are drawn to these three-dimensional snapshots of history, and they expect to see them within military museums. As one youngster exclaimed when he realized that we had removed mannequins from display, he questioned »where are your dummies?« Even when I had explained somewhat ironically that he would have a lifetime to meet or see any number of »dummies«, a successful museum visit to him required that they be out on the floor in some action scene that would help illuminate the subject and space.

Likewise, museums that operate military hardware like the Flying Heritage Collection (p. 58) outside Seattle and the Tank Museum (p. 68) in Bovington, England, along with others that organize events that include reenactors, all attempt to expand the human connection to those military machines. Although perhaps not as accessible as visitors who get rides in Model-T Fords at the Henry Ford Museum, those who attend these events get to see military hardware up-close and in action, and reenactors are sometimes the ones who actively participate.

The need for theatrical installations informs many of the exhibition designs of newer museums even beyond military ones. Nowadays these installations are created by superb designers with talents equal to any prominent architect; some represented within this book are Ralph Appelbaum Associates, Christopher Chadbourne, Event Communications, Gallagher & Associates, Haley Sharpe, the Hettema Group, Kossman.deJong, Luci Creative, and Redman Design. An important extension of the theatricality of their installation designs are IMAX theaters, introductory film presentations, three-dimensional experiences, and interactive electronic programs. All of these are hallmarks of our own age and our own experiences with theme parks, tourist attractions, and personal media devices such as smartphones and tablets. These dynamic interpretive methods are essentially an ultimate outgrowth of antique dioramas and humanity's need to learn about people like us within historic contexts.

### The military museum, today and tomorrow

We have acknowledged the impact that the Imperial War Museum has had on the field of military museums in our era. Likewise, holocaust memorial museums have had an equal impact. They have raised the bar regarding architectural and exhibition design, but also created museum experiences that go beyond objects to expressing the emotive qualities of individual human stories – something that is commonplace today in most military museums. Arguably, the first major museum of this type was the Holocaust Memorial Museum (1993) in Washington, D.C., by James Ingo Freed of I. M. Pei with exhibition installation by Ralph Appelbaum. The emotional content within as well as the professional display drew praise from critics and the general public alike. In terms of pure architectural impact, Daniel Libeskind's Jüdisches Museum (2001) and Peter Eisenman's Holocaust Memorial (2004), both in Berlin, are among the most powerful. Libeskind's angular design (illus. 21) and resultant spaces provide visitors with a disconcerting journey emblematic of the Jewish experience there, and the loss of Jewish cultural contributions to the city, during World War II. Eisenman's maze of 2,711 concrete slabs projects the overwhelming inhumanity of the holocaust. Whether using simplified geometric rectilinear or angular design forms and spaces, most military museums today are part of that overall contemporary pattern, though traditional architectural forms can still be seen in a few recent examples within this volume. And, Libeskind's Berlin commission led to other high-profile museums, including military ones represented in this book, in Manchester and Dresden (see pp. 26, 72).

In the United States, architect Bartholomew Voorsanger designed a series of important pavilions over a multi-year period in recent years for the National World War II Museum in New Orleans (see p. 114). Begun as a D-Day museum, this institution is one of the American leaders in this muse-

21. Jüdisches Museum, Berlin, 2001. Photo: Günter Schneider.
22. Proposed United Arab Emirates National Military Museum, Abu Dhabi, designed 2008 and later. Photo: Voorsanger Architects PC and Voorsanger Architects Archive.
23. The Great Patriotic War Museum, Minsk, Belarus, 2014. Photo: shutterstock.com.
24. Saudi Air Force Museum, Riyadh, 1992 and later, with F-15D gate guard. Photo: Ahmed Said Hassan.

um type, creating a campus of museum, educational, and theater buildings. They make a major cultural tourism contribution to that city with an annual attendance of more than 700,000 visitors. Like figures can be found at the National Museum of the U.S. Air Force outside Dayton (see p. 92) at more than 800,000 visitors each year. Even museums in other suburban locations such as the National Museum of the Marine Corps have an average annual attendance of 500,000. Military museums based in major urban environments fare even better each year, with annual numbers of over a million visitors in such places as the U.S.S. *Midway* Museum in San Diego and the Intrepid Sea, Air & Space Museum in New York (see p. 60). I like to think that with these fairly solid attendances, some of it relates to their striking exhibit and architectural designs, where visitors see that these examples have joined the greater family of how major museums should look and feel today.

### The military museum: more than memorial

What can one say after this brief chronicling of the building type? We have determined that the origins are a bit loosely defined back to collections of war trophies by victorious armies. Examples of militaria and weapons collections date back centuries, and purpose-built structures back at least to 1820. We have seen a few examples where war memorials with museum collections date to the first decades of the twentieth century, mostly as part of an awareness to build useful memorials after the World Wars. And we have seen that this type of museum found itself in more established situations with large-scale buildings in the last decades of the twentieth century.

Museums of this type have been redefining their missions over the past decade or two, with an increasing emphasis nowadays on STEM educational programs – Science, Technology, Engineering and Math – as well as a variety of ways to attract families and repeat visitors. Some find themselves giving back to society by hosting veterans job fairs and supporting military families. And, as with art museums and science centers, all are ramping up their exhibit offerings and customer service attitudes to encourage repeat and new visitation. It is my hope that the pictorial survey which follows will give you a renewed appreciation of how far these museums have come in their architecture and exhibition presentation as they join the family of high-profile museums around the world. Some museums are just finishing up now in 2018/19. These include 3 North's American Civil War Museum in Richmond, Virginia, and the National Veterans Memorial and Museum in Columbus, Ohio by Allied Works architects with exhibits by Ralph Appelbaum Associates. Those in the planning stage, such as Bart Voorsanger's National Military Museum for the United Arab Emirates in Abu Dhabi (illus. 22), and Payette's National Coast Guard Museum and the Medal of Honor Museum by Safdie Architects, both to have exhibits created by Gallagher & Associates, will hopefully join them in construction one day. All demonstrate that creative architecture and exhibition design continues within military museums of the near future.

### A note on the building selection

Museums represented within this survey present a broad range of facilities over the past two decades. They include large and small institutions, museums with static displays and those with operable military equipment, government as well as privately supported organizations, collections that range from housing miniscule memorabilia to »heavy metal« artifacts weighing many tons, and constructions themselves that include historic restorations and renovations, as well as cutting-edge new edifices. Compiling this selection required the diligent cooperation of architects, designers, institutions, and photographers. Museums published here represent their efforts as much as my own.

Unfortunately, not all visually interesting museums could be examined within the pages allocated to this volume. For some, such as the boldly geometric additions of the Mons Memorial Museum (2015) in Belgium by Atelier Pierre Hebbelinck, the intriguingly expressive Great Patriotic War Museum (illus. 23) in Minsk (2014) by Viktor Kramarenko, Leonid Levin, and others, or the artifact-rich Personal Courage Wing of the Museum of Flight in Seattle (2004) by NBBJ and SRJ, with Chris Mailander of the Museum of Flight for exhibition design, it was difficult to locate multiple, high quality views. Likewise, I could not acquire enough visual information to represent two important early aviation museums. One is Flugwerft Schleissheim outside Munich, a World War I era historic aerodrome that was restored and expanded (1992) by Pranschke, Reichert and Maluche. Another is the Royal Saudi Air Force Museum (1992) in Riyadh designed by Marks Barfield and the Zuhair Fayez partnership (illus. 24). This was one of the first new museum installation designs after the Gulf War, by an architect who also went on to create one of London's icons, the Eye. Moreover, several others were elusive to document within the span of creating this book. One is the work of famed architect Arata Isozaki for the Japanese Army Museum (designed 2005) within the Jianchuan Museum Complex in Chengdu, China. The drawings published in *GA Document* (2006) bear no relationship to buildings shown on that museum's website, though the Chinese News Network reported in 2015 that Isozaki had visited the site multiple times, being recorded there in stock photo images, and that he designed a 37,673 square feet (3,500 sq. m) exhibit space.

Those and likely others must await documentation within another volume. I apologize if there are institutions that should have been represented, their exclusion not being intentional. We remind readers, however, that our selection is not intended to be definitive but rather it seeks to demonstrate the range of contemporary design solutions to housing, displaying, and interpreting military history and artifacts. This museum building type joins other museums in the increased sophistication of their exhibition presentations. The selection is arranged chronologically, with projects just finished or under construction at the end of the sequence. In all, these museums and their exhibitions provide the general public and enthusiasts alike with professional design solutions that honor service and sacrifice around the world.

**Bansei Tokko Peace Memorial Museum (originally Kaseda City Peace Memorial Hall), Minamisatsuma City, Kagoshima Prefecture, Japan, 1993**
Tanseishya Co. Ltd. Architects

Although Russian pilots in both World Wars engaged in ramming German aircraft, Japanese aviators towards the end of World War II specialized in such attacks against ships, first seen systematically during the Battle of Leyte Gulf in later October 1944. The kamikaze or divine wind attacks practiced then through the end of the war caused the deaths of more than 7,000 Allied navy personnel at the price of some 3,800 Japanese pilots. The Bansei air base was established late 1944 as one of the last ones constructed for Special Attack or kamikaze pilots. From here they went on missions to Okinawa to protect the Japanese homeland by using these tactics. During the Battle of Okinawa from April to June 1945 some thirty-three naval and cargo ships were sunk or greatly damaged by 1,465 planes whose pilots died while attacking those ships.

In 1972, a memorial was built on the plaza here to commemorate Special Attack pilots who left to die for their country. The museum was opened two decades later. Both were spearheaded by the efforts of Hichiro Naemura, an instructor pilot during the war. Although its appearance relates to an abstracted version of Japanese vernacular forms, it is said to have more particular references to this site and the museum's mission. The angular-braced levels of the building have been compared to those of biplane Yokosuka K5Y trainers nicknamed »red dragonflys«, planes also surprisingly used in some kamikaze attacks. The angled or peaked roof outline is also said to have been related to the silhouette of praying hands and prayers for peace.

Artifacts within the museum contain memorabilia of the 201 soldiers and pilots who died here from American bombing runs over the base, or on Special Attack missions. Their last letters and photos are displayed on the upper floor walls and cases. The main floor recounts the history of the base and features the wreckage of a rare Aichi E13A floatpane. It crash-landed about 1,968 feet (600 m) offshore on June 4, 1945 after returning from a reconnaissance mission over Okinawa. It was salvaged in 1992 from a depth of some 16 feet (5 m) and prepared for exhibition by the aviation workshop at Kanoya Air Base. Perhaps equally important is a photograph from May 26, 1945 which shows young Special Attack pilots based here, before they depart on their final mission.

The museum building is a relatively small one at more than 6,114 square feet (568 sq. m), but it witnesses more than 12,000 visitors each year. The Tanseishya Co. architectural firm has a long history, founded 1946 and renamed to its current one in 1959. Since then it has established offices around Japan, specializing mostly in retail and food service interiors. These include the food court at Haneda Airport's international terminal, various Subway restaurants, and McDonald's new generation stores in Japan. Recent museum work includes the Toyota Commemorative Museum of Industry and Technology (2010), and the Scmaglev and Railway Park (2011), both in Aichi.

1. Museum and memorial (right). Photo: Bansei Tokko Peace Museum.
2. Bansei's kamikaze or Special Attack pilots, 1945. Photo: Wikipedia.
3. Aichi Type 0/E13A Reconnaissance Seaplane, captured on Kwajalein in the Marshall Islands, photographed 1944. Photo: National Archives.
4. Interior of the museum displaying salvaged Aichi Type 0 Reconnaissance Seaplane. Photo: Bansei Tokko Peace Museum.

A23

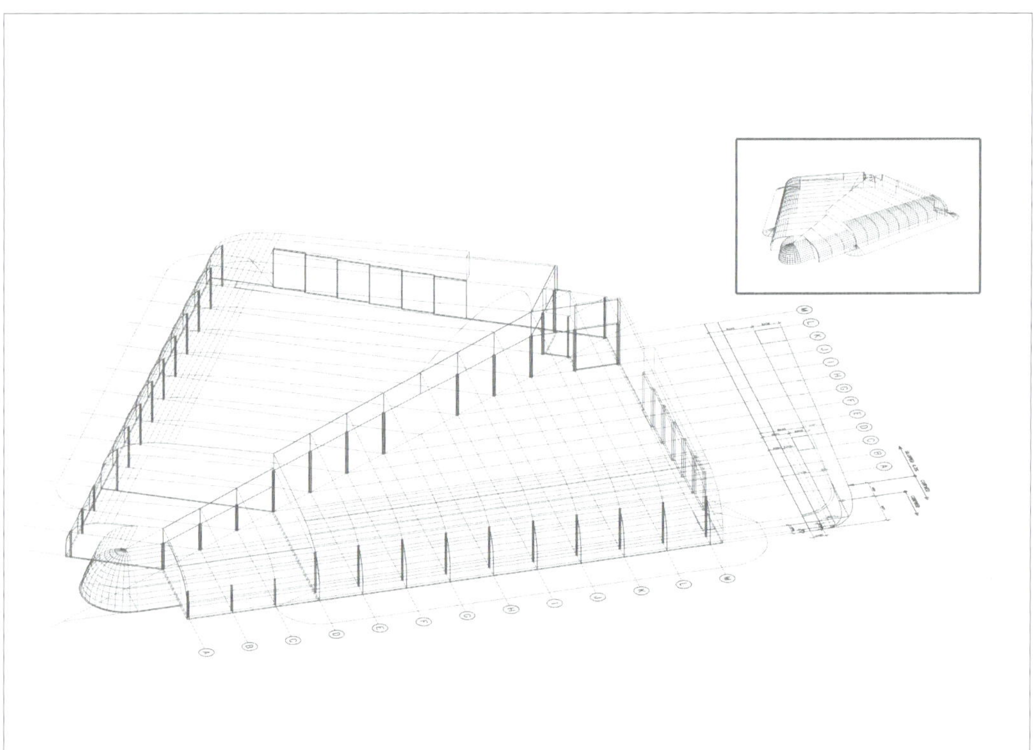

**Canadian Warplane Heritage Museum, Hamilton, Ontario, Canada, 1996**
Chamberlain Architect Services

Founded 1972/73 by Dennis Bradley, Alan Ness, Peter Matthews, and John Weir, the four friends purchased their first aircraft, a Fairey Firefly. The collection grew within a hangar at Hamilton's John C. Munro International Airport. A 1993 fire provided the opportunity to rebuild its facility into a purpose-built museum. The Canadian Warplane Heritage Museum collects and even operates aircraft formerly flown by Canadian armed forces from World War II through the present. Its collection, thus, includes mostly Canadian variants of British and American aircraft. Members can reserve flights within some operable historic aircraft from trainers such as a Boeing Stearman, de Havilland Chipmunk or Tiger Moth, or North American Harvard (AT-6 Texan), or bombers such as a rare Avro Lancaster Mk.X. Acquired 1977, this plane was originally manufactured in Malton, Canada, in July 1945. It was restored and flew again in 1988. Of the 7,300 built only seventeen survive today, and only two of them are operable – this and one in England. In addition to flyable planes, vintage aircraft from World War II through the jet age are displayed throughout. The 1996 construction that houses the museum was designed by Brian Chamberlain, an architect since 1978 and himself a pilot and Canadian air force veteran.

Inspired by streamlined aircraft components, Chamberlain created a curvilinear, stealth-like, delta-wing shape for the museum. It is located at the southeast corner of the airport's grounds. He designed two interlocking triangular open spaces, that create 80,000 square feet (7,432 sq. m) of hangar space for their collection of some fifty aircraft. The curved roof trusses provide up to 210 feet (64 m) of exhibit and aircraft space below. The airside elevation at the north side of the delta-shape provides aircraft access to the apron, taxiways and runways. Landscaped berms surround the structure on the other sides. The program also provided space for static exhibits, workshop, museum store, offices, gallery, educational center, as well as a lounge and café.

Brian Chamberlain's firm has designed a number of buildings (see entry for the Juno Beach Centre, p. 30), including works in his own city of Burlington, Ontario as well as Tim Horton's Children's Foundation Camps in Canada and the United States. His other aviation-related works include the Jetport hangar, Cargo Centre, and Transport Canada facilities at Hamilton International Airport and the air traffic control tower at Toronto's Pearson International Airport. His design team works on a number of hotels and restaurants as well, even beyond Canada.

1. Aerial view. Photo: Jan Waginski.
2. Axonometric view. Photo: Chamberlain Architect Services Limited.
3. Night view of CF-104 Starfighter as the museum gate guard. Photo: Jan Waginski.
4. Museum interior showing training aircraft in the foreground, with Lancaster and B-25 bombers in the background. Photo: Jan Waginski.

**American Air Museum of the Imperial War Museum, Duxford, England, 1997**
Foster Associates (today Foster + Partners); exhibition design: Redman Design

Duxford Aerodrome dates to World War I in 1918, almost 60 miles (96.5 km) northeast of London. It was an important base for Royal Air Force/ RAF and American Army Air Force squadrons in World War II. After the war, the RAF operated in the early jet age when the single concrete runway was created 1949–51, though RAF operations ceased there a decade later. In 1968 it was used for one of the locations within the feature film *Battle of Britain* as well as the 1989 film *Memphis Belle*. As part of its expansion program, the Imperial War Museum/IWM acquired the site from the Ministry of Defence in 1976. In 2008 the IWM acquired the rights to much of the surrounding property as well. Facilities adjacent to the runway are used by the IWM as well as the Duxford Aviation Society, a non-profit organization that maintains an extensive civil aviation collection here, and operators of historic aircraft such as »Classic Wings« and the »Fighter Collection«. The buildings are of historic significance dating back to World War I, with some new additions to the airport's landscape. One such is the American Air Museum of the Imperial War Museum, an award-winning exhibition space designed by Lord Norman Foster. It is sited on the southwest side of the row of hangars and display areas used by the IWM and its partners here.

Foster, an RAF veteran as well as a pilot, created this great masterpiece of aviation museum design from 1987 to 1997. The aircraft-like nose shape of the hangar was constructed with precast concrete panels. They shape a space of some 79,652 square feet (7,400 sq. m) housing what is likely the best American aircraft collection outside the United States. The building was created in response to the program to accommodate the size of a B-52. Ramps at the interior's perimeter give more than 350,000 visitors annually a walking tour of American military aviation from World War I through the jet age Cold War. Concrete panels above contain hanging points from which to rig the aircraft. The glazed wall facing south to the runway provides ample light as well as a spectacular window from which to watch airshows. The building itself is constructed within a landscape berm. Visitors access it from a north entry, as if one enters a bunker or revetment-like hangar on a military base. Etched glass panels flanking the entry are a memorial to American airmen who died in World War II. Created by artist Renato Niemis and entitled *Counting the Cost*, it depicts 7,031 American planes etched on 52 glass panels, representing those crews missing in action during World War II. The museum displays were revamped in 2015/16 to include artifacts of some 85 individuals, most of which have never been exhibited before, in a £ 3 million project supported by the Historic Lottery Fund.

Foster's American Air Museum earned the 1998 Stirling Prize Royal Institute of British Architects Building of the Year Award. The jury cited »the elegant engineered form of the building and the technically driven shapes of the aeroplanes. The building itself sustains the fascination of these objects«. Foster has created iconic buildings around the world, from skyscrapers such as Commerzbank in Frankfurt (1996) and the Swiss RE Tower (2003) in London, to airport terminals in London Stansted (1991) and Hong Kong International (1998), to public buildings such as Berlin's Reichstag (1999). But he has also designed subsequent buildings to house aviation treasures, from Fortaleza Hall (2010) in Racine, Wisconsin, to the renovation of the Imperial War Museum (2014) in London (see p. 80).

1. Plan. Photo: Foster+Partners.
2. Section. Photo: Foster+Partners.
3. Museum exterior landside. Photo: ©Nigel Young. Foster+Partners.

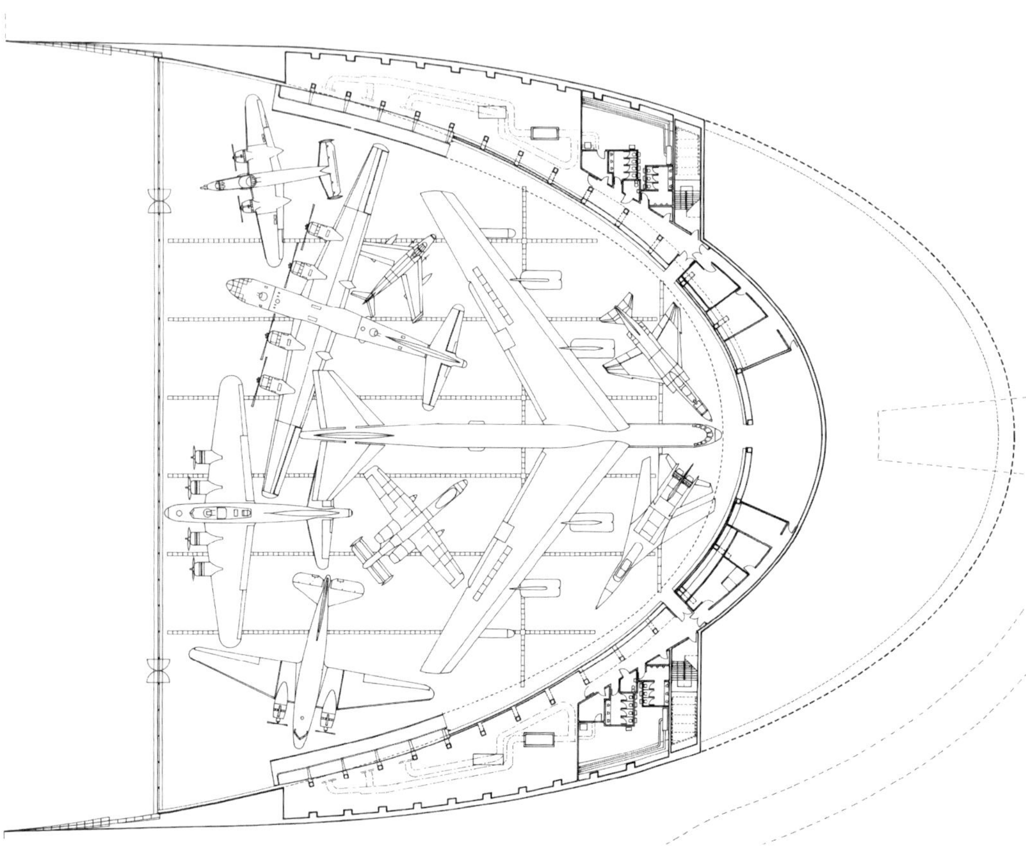

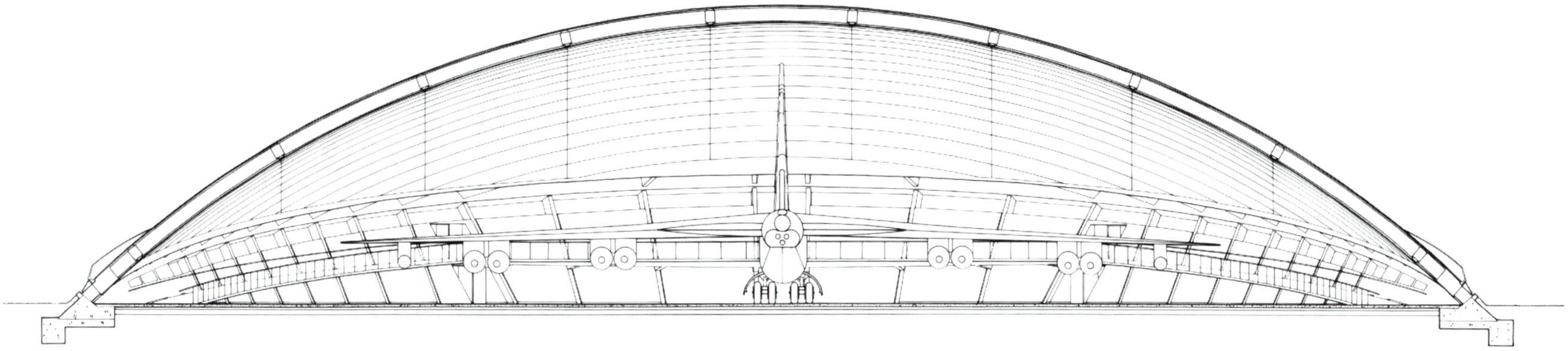

4. Museum interior showing glazed wall airside, with Grumman TBM Avenger hung above a North American PBJ-1, a naval version of the B-25.
5. Museum exterior from the airside, and the tail of a Handley Page Victor bomber.
6. Museum interior showing A-10 with Stearman trainer hung above.
All photos: ©Nigel Young, Foster+Partners.

**Pacific Aviation Museum, Ford Island, Pearl Harbor, Hawaii, USA, 1999 and later**
Glenn E. Mason

»Yesterday, December seventh, 1941, a date which will live in infamy, the United States of America was suddenly and deliberately attacked by naval and air forces of the Empire of Japan.« So said President Franklin Delano Roosevelt in his famed radio address. Thirty-three minutes afterwards, Congress declared war on Japan. The day after the raid, American losses were counted as twenty-one ships sunk or greatly damaged, 164 aircraft lost and another 159 damaged, and 2,390 killed, 49 being civilians. The Japanese lost 29 planes and counted 64 dead with five small midget submarines sunk during the raid. The battle cry »Remember Pearl Harbor« was one that resounded throughout the next four years of the conflict, until the formal Japanese surrender on the deck of the battleship U.S.S. *Missouri* in Tokyo Bay, on September 2, 1945. When one visits Pearl Harbor today, they can see tangible artifacts of the beginning and end of America's involvement in that conflict.

The first and most important of these is the submerged ruined hull of the battleship *Arizona*, sunk in that attack. Of the 1,177 sailors and marines who died aboard, over 900 could not be recovered. The site is considered a national cemetery. The 1962 memorial above designed by Alfred Preis acts as an open-air chapel from which visitors can contemplate those sacrifices made by all who died in the attack. About 5,000 visit the shrine daily, accessed by naval launch. Moored nearby on Ford Island is the former battleship *Missouri,* now open as the Battleship Missouri Memorial. The ship was commissioned June 11, 1944 and in service, on and off, essentially through Operation Desert Storm, until being decommissioned March 31, 1992. The ship became a museum in 1998. *Missouri* was one of four Iowa-class battleships (*Iowa*, *New Jersey*, and *Wisconsin* being the others) built in World War II that are now museum ships. The Iowa class were the largest American battleships ever built with a crew of 2,700 and nine sixteen-inch guns, though the class was smaller than the Japanese super-battleships *Yamato* and *Musashi* (see Yamato Museum entry, p. 38). In addition to those two naval vessels the Pearl Harbor Visitor Center contains the U.S.S. *Bowfin* Submarine Museum and Park.

Also on Ford Island is the Pacific Aviation Museum, established 1999, with buildings that were part of the Naval Air Station. The historic hangars and control tower are being restored as part of a public-private partnership since the base is still active. During the attack, Ford Island had dozens of PBY Catalina patrol planes that were destroyed, as well as being the home to American aircraft carriers that were out of port when the attack took place. The 158 feet (48 m) high control tower was unfinished at the time but was completed May 1, 1942. Its restored red and white paint scheme dates from the 1960s, the tower previously painted in various gray camouflage schemes. The museum has a multi-year master plan for restoring three historic hangars and auxiliary buildings such as the control tower, all in a 16 acres (6.47 ha) site. Hangar 37 from 1939 of 7.25 acres (2.93 ha) is restored and opened 2007 as part of the phase 1 repairs, along with the control tower which is in the process of being restored so that visitors can access it. Hangar 79 is 86,000 square feet (7,990 sq. m) and still has bullet holes from the 1941 attack. It is open as a restoration shop, in an effort to raise funds for its conversion into the World War II display area. When that phase is implemented, hangar 54 will be the next exhibit area to be developed, dedicated to post-war aerospace in the jet age and Cold War.

1. Aerial view in 1984 of Ford Island, at the lower right the U.S.S. *Arizona* Memorial offshore. The lower left shows the aircraft carrier U.S.S. *Enterprise* (CVN-65). Photo: National Archives.
2. Restored control tower, Ford Island, Pacific Aviation Museum. Photo: shutterstock.com.
3. Restored exhibition hangar 37, Pacific Aviation Museum, showing North American B-25 Mitchell bomber in the foreground. Photo: shutterstock.com.
4.Aerial view in 1991 with the U.S.S. *Arizona* Memorial off the northeast end of Ford Island. Photo: National Archives.

**Battle of Midway Exhibition, Midway International Airport, Chicago, Illinois, USA, 2001–07**

A. Epstein and Sons (today Epstein), ARTN and DMAC Architecture

Although essentially the railroad and then commercial aviation hub of the United States, Chicago has always been a Navy town despite not being on the Atlantic or Pacific coasts. Its location on Lake Michigan secured that connotation. There are a number of tangible architectural and historic associations here. The Navy has had several cruisers and now a submarine named after Chicago during the late nineteenth and twentieth centuries. More important, the expansive Great Lakes Naval Station (1911) north of Chicago was planned and built by architect Jarvis Hunt. Numerous additions were made over the twentieth century (see p. 48), making it the largest Navy basic training base in the nation at some 1,628 acres (658.8 ha). Glenview Naval Air Station northwest of Chicago was a Curtiss Wright airport taken over by the Navy, even before World War II, to train pilots. The Navy expanded the airport beyond the now historic Hangar One built 1929 for the Curtiss facility. The base was closed 1995 and the land redeveloped. Chicago's Municipal Pier (1916) by Charles S. Frost, renamed Navy Pier in 1927 to commemorate veterans of World War I, was used as a naval training center during World War II. At that time, Navy Pier was the home port of two side-wheel steamers converted into aircraft carriers – the U.S.S. *Sable* and *Wolverine* – both used for pilot qualification training. The most famous naval aviator who trained here was President George H.W. Bush. On an interesting archaeological note, more than 200 World War II Navy planes remain at the bottom of Lake Michigan as part of this training effort, several salvaged and restored as museum artifacts.

With this Navy-centered background in mind, it comes as no surprise when, soon after the end of World War II, Chicago's two major commercial airports were officially named after a naval aviation hero and heroic battle focused on naval aviation. O'Hare International Airport was officially named in 1949 after Edward »Butch« O'Hare, the Navy's first ace when he earned the Congressional Medal of Honor in 1942 for shooting down Japanese bombers attacking his aircraft carrier, the U.S.S. *Lexington*. A restored Grumman F4F-3 Wildcat aircraft, salvaged from Lake Michigan, is on display in Terminal 2 there, painted in the markings of O'Hare's plane. Chicago's earlier Municipal Airport was renamed Midway International Airport in 1949 after the naval aviation Battle of Midway fought June 4–7, 1942, which historians believe to be the turning point of war in the Pacific. The Chicago Marine Heritage Society wanted to commemorate that historic battle with an exhibit at Chicago's Midway airport that would parallel the display done slightly earlier at O'Hare.

The plane often associated with that battle is the Douglas SBD Dauntless dive bomber, credited with sinking four of Japan's aircraft carriers. Working with salvager A+T Recovery, the Society led the team to secure an aircraft from the Naval Aviation Museum at Pensacola, Florida, for restoration and display at the newly opened Midway terminal (2004). The building was designed by HNTB with A. Epstein and Son as the associate architects. Epstein worked with the Society as well as with artist Ellen Sandor of ARTN to prepare the interpretive exhibition under the historic aircraft positioned within Concourse A of the new building. The tiny aluminum clad kiosk of under 100 square feet (9.29 sq. m) serves as memorial chapel of sorts, its interior four walls containing four large colored holograms that are collages of people and events related to the battle. The kiosk was created 2001, situated at slightly different places in the concourse, being recently restored 2017, whereas the Dauntless Dive bomber was installed in 2007.The Society coordinated the project implementation regarding fundraising with the Navy League of the United States, Chicago Council, who continues to manage and update the exhibition.

1. *Battle of Midway Memorial Collage*, a hologram by ARTN within the four walls of the kiosk interior. Photo: ARTN.
2. Exhibition in Concourse A showing suspended Douglas SBD dive bomber. Photo: courtesy Epstein, Ballogg Photography.
3. Kiosk within the exhibition in 2001. Photo: ARTN.

HE TECHNOLOGY
CONNECTION
Concourse A
A1
A2
A3

Telephones

**Imperial War Museum North, Manchester, England, 2002**

Daniel Libeskind; exhibition design: Event and Real Studios

After a competition among several sites within northern England to host this new branch of the Imperial War Museum/IWM, the museum chose the site along the Manchester Ship Canal. This was done, in part, because of that city's industrial heritage during World War II as well as it being bombed during the Blitz, 1940. The museum then held a 1997 competition, selecting Polish-born American architect Daniel Libeskind to design the building. Libeskind created a design where three major components of the building represented three interconnected curved aluminum clad shards of a globe shattered by conflict – air, earth, and water. An anecdote used to describe this was Libeskind putting a teapot into a plastic bag, dropping it from his window, and using the broken pieces as a design source.

The 180 feet (55 m) high air shard houses the museum entrance, education space, and a viewing platform whereas the earth shard contains most of the museum galleries, and the water shard includes service spaces such as a café and entertaining space along the canal. The curved and angular spaces within relate to their exterior shapes. These were intentionally designed to be disconcerting to the visitor in a way that angular spaces at Libeskind's Jewish Museum in Berlin represent unsettling historic moments. The museum's exhibitions within the earth shard include permanent galleries in the main space, both chronological and thematic. Larger artifacts range from a Soviet T-34/85 tank to an AV-8B Harrier, a British jet used by the United States Marine Corps, and twisted steel beams from the World Trade Center in New York, destroyed by terrorist attack on September 11, 2001. The white walls in the main gallery act as screens for image projection, making the space itself a dynamic historic photomontage called *The Big Picture Show*. The museum, with support from the Arts Council, has also been commissioning fine art since 2010. These include Gerry Judah's sculpture of a war-torn landscape titled *The Crusader* (2010) and Chava Rosenzweig's ceramic stars of David titled *A star shall stride from Jacob and a sceptre bearer shall rise* (2013). Beyond permanent installation, temporary galleries are also housed within the earth shard.

The building itself came in well under budget at £ 28.5 million instead of the planned £ 40 million. Its first year witnessed more than 470,000 visitors, hitting the one million mark by August 2005. Libeskind's design received critical acclaim by the public and professionals alike. In 2009, the museum selected the firm of Topotek 1 to develop the exterior spaces of the site in a way that are visually compatible with the dynamic building. As such, camouflage patterns and landscape elevation changes were used as a source of inspiration for their work. This artistic landscaping was not implemented.

1. View from across the Manchester Ship Canal. Photo © Bitter Bredt, Jan Bitter Fotografie.
2. Main or gallery-floor plan. Photo: © Studio Daniel Libeskind.
3. Ground-floor plan. Photo: © Studio Daniel Libeskind.

pp. 28, 29
4, 5. Gallery view and air-shard viewing platform. Photos: © Bitter Bredt, Jan Bitter Fotografie.

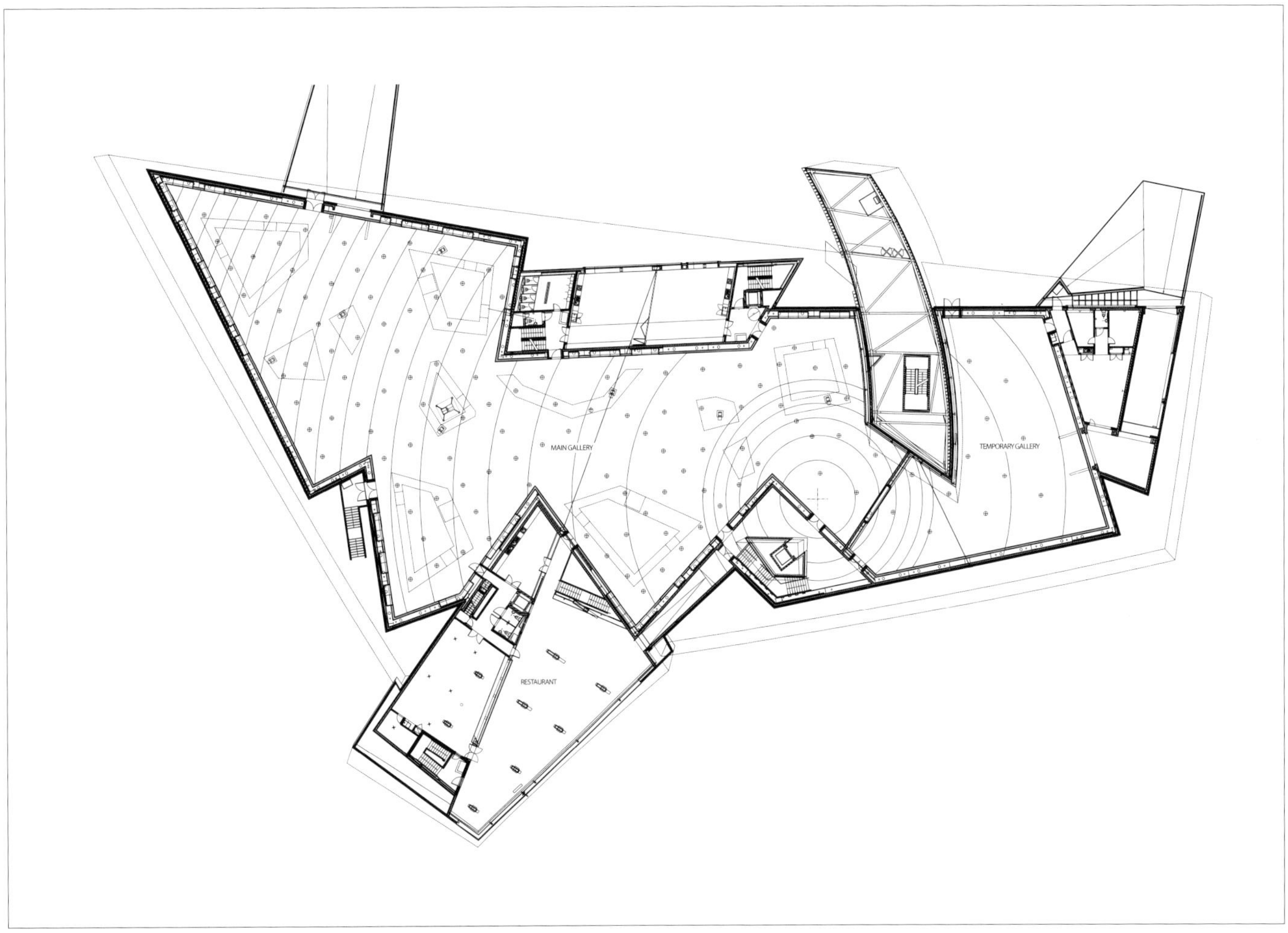
MAIN GALLERY
TEMPORARY GALLERY
RESTAURANT

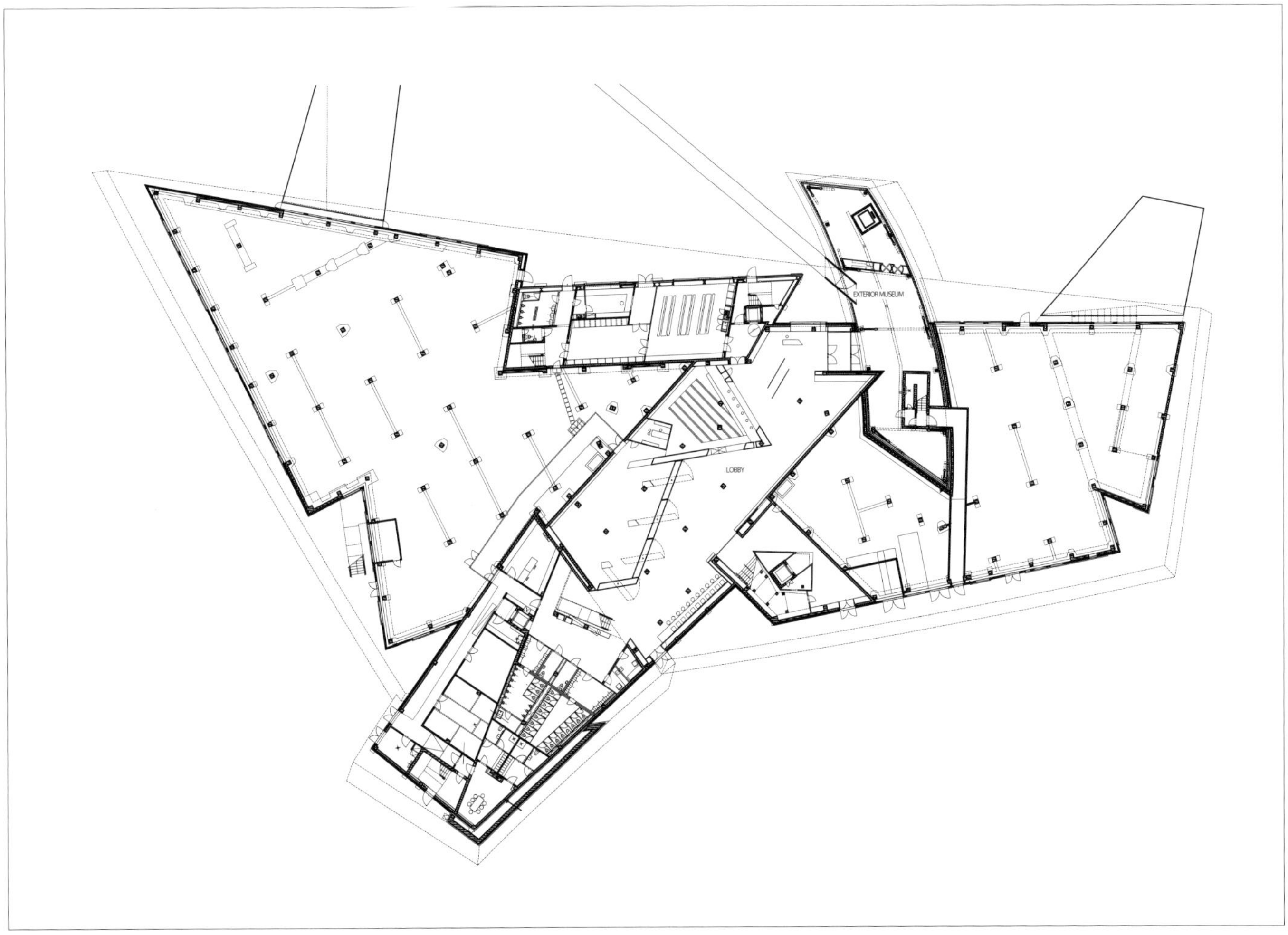
EXTERIOR MUSEUM
LOBBY

**Juno Beach Centre, Courseulles-sur-Mer, Normandy, France, 2003**
Chamberlain Architect Services

The Juno Beach Centre provides us with a tangible commemorative structure of Canada's participation in the liberation of France on D-Day, June 6, 1944. In 2017 more than 85,000 visitors came to the Juno Beach Centre to see their exhibitions and participate in events for Canada Day every July 1, as well as a variety of commemorative concerts and ceremonies to honor the sacrifice their service personnel made on the beaches of Normandy in World War II. Of the 135,000 Allies who participated in the June 6 invasion, 14,000 were Canadians. The 3rd Canadian Infantry Division and the 2nd Canadian Armoured Brigade assaulted Juno Beach, and captured coastal towns of Graye-sur-Mer, Courseulles-sur-Mer, Bernières-sur-Mer and part of Saint-Aubin-sur-Mer. Garth Webb, as well as a group of Canadian veterans and their families, all spearheaded a 1990s campaign to create a memorial center near the very beach that witnessed these heroic deeds. In a public-private partnership of the Canadian and French governments as well as individual donations, the group raised enough to construct the center at a cost of $ 10 million Canadian. Additional support for its continued functioning comes through donations to the Juno Beach Association.

The building's site consists of 3.7 acres (1.5 ha), the structure itself covering 15,392 square feet (1,430 sq. m). Brian Chamberlain, who earlier designed the Canadian Warplane Museum (see p. 16), created this gem of a building in a pentagonal form that reflects both the basic structure of a Canadian Maple Leaf symbol as well as the shape of a military award, the Order of Canada. The angular shapes and curves are clad in titanium with glazing on the same plane as the cladding, the actual building structure being of steel and concrete. Exhibits within include a 7,000 square feet (650 sq. m) permanent display on Canada's efforts during the war along with a related film, and an exhibit about Canada today. Temporary exhibitions are located in a 1,600 square feet (149 sq. m) space. A smaller 1,400 square feet (130 sq. m) space is used for educational programs and school groups. Tours of the center also include guided tours of Juno Park and the remains of Atlantic Wall fortifications nearby. Colin Gibson created the bronze abstracted figural sculpture outside, entitled *Remembrance and Renewal*, the location being used for official ceremonies related to D-Day anniversaries and the center. The center was officially opened June 6, 2003.

1. Aerial view on the English Channel. Photo: Damien Letorey, courtesy Chamberlain Architect Services, Ltd.
2. Façade. Photo: Damien Letorey, courtesy Chamberlain Architect Services, Ltd.
3. Interior exhibits. Photo: Juno Beach Centre Association.

Shhh,
Someone May be
THE WALLS HAVE EARS

**Canadian War Museum, Ottawa, Canada, 2005**
Moriyama & Teshima Architects, Griffith Rankin Cook; exhibition design: Haley Sharpe and Origin Studios

The museum began its life as a collection of military artifacts in 1880. This formed the basis of the Canadian War Museum, officially established 1942 in an existing location not appropriate to its growing collection and potential audience. Its real opportunity came in the 1990s with plans to relocate the museum into a new facility within the parliamentary district of Ottawa. A 2001 Request for Information produced a further Request for a Proposal from the team of Moriyama & Teshima of Toronto who partnered with Ottawa-based Griffith Rankin Cook. Their team was tasked with a fast track schedule for this large museum facility, starting in November 2001 with completion expected for a grand opening on May 8, 2005 – the sixtieth anniversary of VE day/Victory in Europe day.

This was an amazing opportunity for designer Raymond Moriyama who, as a young man, found himself within a Canadian internment camp after the Japanese attack on Pearl Harbor, December 7, 1941, and widespread fears about a Japanese invasion of the American and Canadian west coast. He recounted his journey within *In Search of a Soul* (2006), in which he described his experience designing and building this project. Moriyama cited his process in terms of interviewing a wide range of Canadians about their expectations for the building as well as bringing some of his own observations to the site. These include the importance of having the building reflect landscapes scarred by war as well as Canada's own vast landscape, and also having a sacred place for Remembrance Day, November 11, marking the armistice of World War I.

Moriyama's team created a design masterwork. They made a building that incorporates concrete bunker-like walls, powerful gallery and especially contemplative space within both Regeneration Hall and Memorial Hall, along with a large publicly accessible storage in LeBreton Gallery for military vehicles and machinery. Their building is situated in a berm into the landscape in Le Breton Flats as a giant symbol of regeneration in its green roof. Exhibits within were designed by Haley Sharpe from Leicester in England and Ottawa's Origin Studios. They present visitors with a mixed media experience, theatrical lighting and sets, all related to dramatic stories and an overall feeling of rebirth after conflict. Exhibit forms and space often parallel the angular architectural forms of the building with spartan materials, rough textures, and like color tones used in both exhibit and building. Exhibits are organized into theme sections regarding military events throughout Canada's centuries old history.

There is also a dedicated space for the Royal Canadian Legion of Honor focusing on maquettes for the Canadian War Memorial at Vimy Ridge (1936) by Walter Seymour Allward. In addition to gallery spaces and memorial or regenerative ones, the museum has an important military history research center and also a large war art collection.

When completed, Moriyama wrote that construction costs came in at $ 218 Canadian per square foot, considerably under the average cost of local museums buildings then which were more like $ 300 per square foot. Internationally building a museum then cost almost twice that. All told, his museum contains 440,000 square feet (40,877 sq. m) sitting within a landscaped site of 18.5 acres (7.5 ha). It received numerous design awards in Canada, Britain and Ireland when completed.

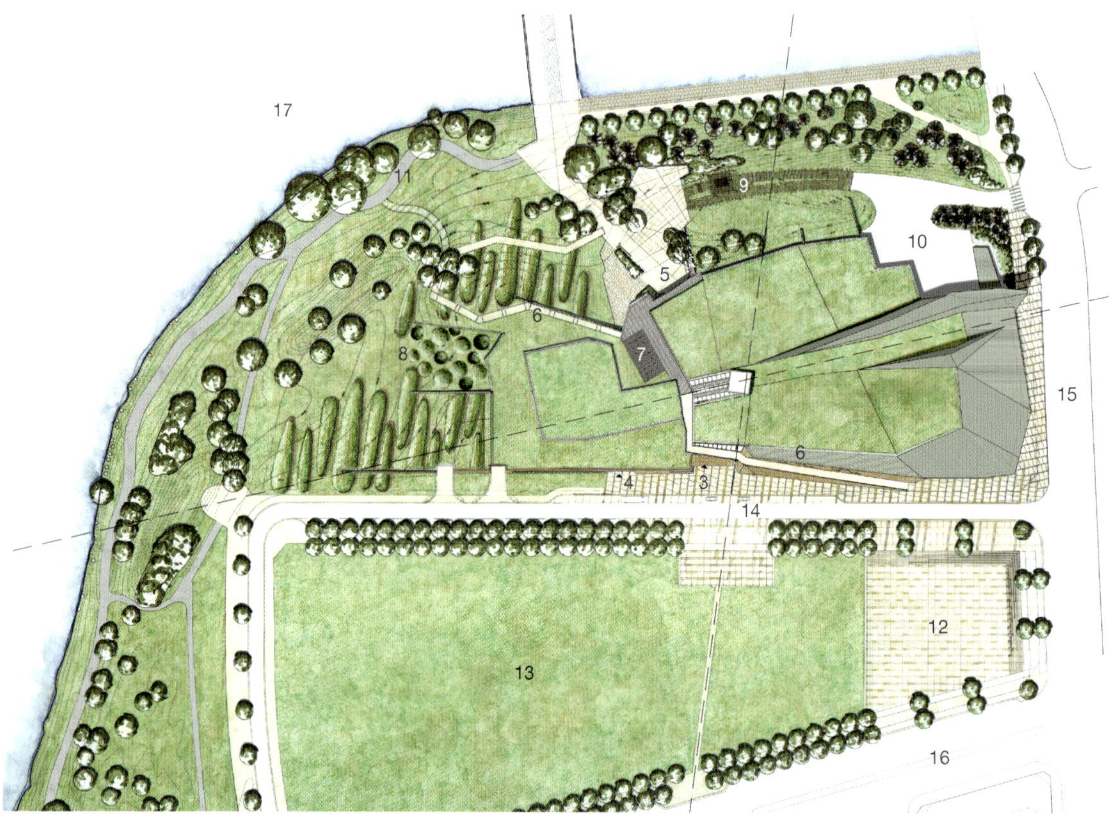


1 peace tower axis
2 remembrance day axis
3 main entrance
4 group entrance
5 north entrance
6 la traverse
7 memorial garden
8 field of memories
9 demonstration track
10 service yard
11 trans canada trail
12 parade square
13 the commons
14 vimy street
15 booth street
16 ottawa river parkway
17 ottawa river

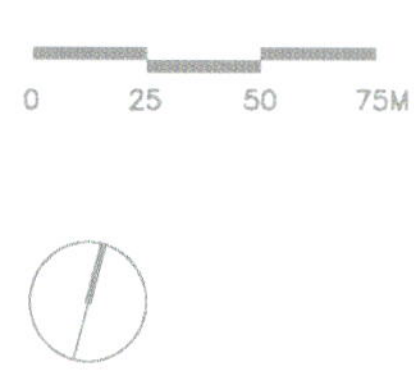

1. Site Plan. Photo: Moriyama and Teshima.
2. Museum from the east. Photo: Harry Foster © Canadian War Museum CWM2014-0025-0001-Dp2.
3. South wall. Photo: ©Tom Arban Photography Inc.

pp.34, 35
4. Exterior wall of the Memorial Hall within the museum's lobby. Photo: ©Tom Arban Photography Inc.
5. Interior of the Memorial Hall on November 11, Remembrance Day. Photo: Harry Foster © Canadian War Museum CWM2011-0050-0004-Dp2.
6. CF-101 Voodoo Interceptor in the LeBreton Gallery. Photo: Harry Foster © Canadian War Museum CWM2012-0032-0003-Dm.
7. »The Cold War Twilight«, Canadian Experience Gallery 4, showing Russian T-72 tank. Photo: Marie-Louise Deruaz © Canadian War Museum CWM2012-0070-0002-Dm.

002

WALLS ARE NOT EVERLASTING !

**Museum of Science and Industry, Chicago, Illinois, USA. Housing of *U-505*, 2005**
Lohan Caprile Goettsch Associates (today Goettsch Partners); exhibition design: Christopher Chadbourne & Associates

Just about every child in Chicago knows the Museum of Science and Industry with its famed Coal Mine Exhibition, essentially dating back to the 1933 Century of Progress Exposition, as well as its model railroad exhibit tracing a trip from Chicago to Seattle, and Hollywood star Colleen Moore's Fairy Castle model. The museum itself is a reconstruction of the Fine Arts Building from the World's Columbian Exposition (1893), originally designed by Charles Atwood of D.H. Burnham and Co. The museum still has the brick interior walls used when it was the fair's fine arts structure, but the classical lath and plaster exteriors were replaced by masonry ones in the interwar years.

Besides being often perceived as a children's playground, with an annual attendance of 1.5 million each year, this museum has important artifacts related to the history of technology, such as the streamlined Burlington Zephyr train (1934). As regards military-related artifacts, two come immediately to mind, both being important war booty. One is a rare Junkers Ju-87R2 dive bomber captured in Libya in 1941 displayed within their transportation exhibition. It was recently restored 2015. This toured the United States in a British war exhibition and remained in Chicago afterwards. Likewise, the *U-505* is a Type IXc German U-boat that was captured by the U.S. Navy on June 4, 1944. The almost 252 feet (76.80 m) long, Hamburg-built, submarine was given to the museum in 1954. It is officially a war memorial dedicated to all sailors who lost their lives in the battles of the Atlantic in both World Wars.

In the later 1990s the submarine, exhibited outside the museum, was in need of restoration. While this was being done, an underground concrete museum building was being created for its eventual display, looking very much as if it were a submarine pen. The new space is 300 feet long by 75 feet wide and 42 feet deep (91.44 x 22.86 x 12.80 m). Before it was completed and covered with a lawn, the U-boat was positioned on massive hydraulic dollies and moved into its exhibition hall by NORSAR Inc., over a multi-day period in April 2004. This project cost over $ 35 million and has over 35,000 square feet (3,252 sq. m) of exhibition space. Interactive exhibits were created by Christopher Chadbourne and Luci Creative, among others, and other artifacts can be seen related to the capture and history of the U-boat. The museum itself offers tours through the U-boat that are experiential for the visitor. But, in a way, nothing compares to its architectural adventure in 2004 some sixty years after its capture, when after restoration and re-positioning, it was open to the public on June 5, 2005.

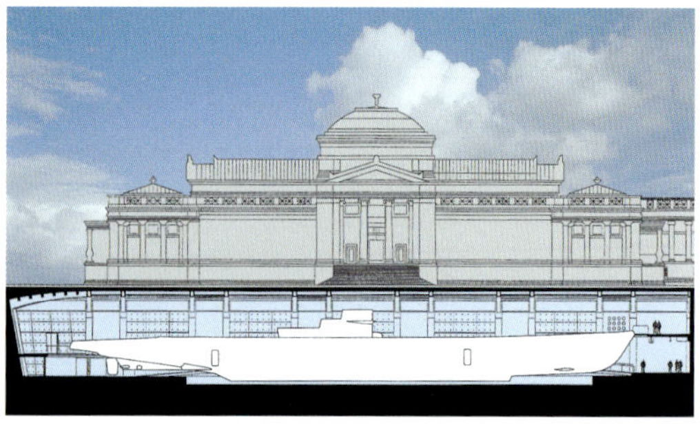

1. Museum elevation with exhibition gallery section below. Photo: © Goettsch Partners.
2. Museum from the northeast. Photo: Mark Ballogg © Steinkamp-Ballogg Photography, courtesy Goettsch Partners.
3. *U-505* within its concrete pen under construction. Photo: © Goettsch Partners.
4, 5. *U-505* final installation and lower level exhibits. Photos: Jon Miller © Hedrich Blessing, courtesy Goettsch Partners.

**Yamato Museum or Kure Maritime Museum, Kure City, Hiroshima Prefecture, Japan, 2005**
Kume Sekkei Co., Ltd.

The battleship *Yamato* is legendary to anyone who has even a cursory knowledge of World War II. The name is so synonymous with a mega warship that *Space Battleship Yamato*, a science fiction Anime series, was developed 1974/75. *Yamato* itself was the brainchild of Rear Admiral Shingo Ishikawa, designed in the mid-1930s to be a class of super battleship. It would be larger and more powerful than any the United States could build that had to transit the Panama Canal from east coast shipyards. The Japanese planned four such giants of some 69,000 tons (62,595,747 kg) carrying eighteen-inch guns. Only three were built after 1937 – the battleships *Yamato* and *Musashi*, along with the *Shinano*. The last was planned as a battleship but converted into an aircraft carrier, after the Japanese lost four carriers in the 1942 Battle of Midway. By contrast, the American *Iowa* class of battleships, developed just before America's entry into World War II with four ships launched 1943/44, had a displacement of only 45,000 tons (40,823,313 kg) and carried sixteen-inch guns.

The supposedly unsinkable super battleships *Musashi* and *Yamato* and their sister ship *Shinano* met their fate 1944/45. *Musashi* was sunk in the Battle of Leyte Gulf on October 24, 1944 after being hit by some twenty torpedoes and seventeen bombs. Its wreck was located by a 2015 expedition financed by Microsoft co-founder Paul Allen, who also created the Flying Heritage Collection (see p. 58). *Shinano* was sunk on November 29, 1944 from four torpedoes fired by the submarine U.S.S. *Archerfish* (SS 311). *Yamato* was sunk on April 7, 1945 by at least eleven torpedoes and six bombs dropped by carrier aircraft during the Battle of Okinawa. The wreckage was discovered 1982–84 and video-surveyed 2015.

The *Yamato* was built in the Kure Naval Arsenal, a shipyard founded 1895 that still functions today through Japan Marine United. It is also the home port for several destroyers and submarines from the Japan Maritime Self Defense Forces/ JMSDF. Two museums related to that history were built side by side on the waterfront. One is the JMSDF museum with its prominent artifact being the decommissioned 1986 submarine SS579 *Akishio* on their plaza. The other is the Kure Maritime Museum, informally known as the Yamato Museum. This brick (brick being a nod to local buildings), glass and concrete multi-level museum of 103,635 square feet (9,628 sq. m) contains artifacts and exhibits related to the history of shipbuilding and World War II. Naturally it focuses on the yard's most important product, the *Yamato*.

The centerpiece artifact on the main floor atrium is a spectacular 1/10 scale model of the famed battleship. This was created with drawings by Masami Aoki, research by Keisuke Hayashi of the Total Media Development Institute Co., Ltd., and construction supervision of Toshiaki Ohshita, chief carpenter of the Yamamoto Shipyard Co., Ltd. Oshita himself, a carpenter with service back to the war years at the shipyard, laid the wooden deck of the model, with approximately 4,000 little pieces of 1/2 inch (15 mm) wood. Yamamoto is the firm who built this model. It is a company established in 1929 that today focuses on repair work for the JMSDF. Even with all the research compiled, some interpretation was necessary. Mr. Takeda of the Yamamoto Shipyard Co. estimated the rudder's shape, which was confirmed after the *Musashi* wreck was discovered and filmed. This amazing model took two years to build and was finished shortly before the museum's opening April 23, 2005, being recently repaired 2017. It is approximately 85 feet (26 m) long, 13 feet (4 m) wide, and weighs about 29 tons (26,308 kg).

1. Battleship *Yamato*, October 30, 1941. Photo: National Archives.
2. North or entry façade of the museum showing, in the plaza, deck gun and propeller artifacts salvaged from the battleship *Mitsu*. Beyond these is the 1986 submarine SS-579 *Akishio*, part of the collection of the adjacent Japanese Maritime Self Defense Force's submarine museum. Photo: courtesy Kure Maritime Museum/Yamato Museum.
3, 4. Battleship *Yamato* model within the main-floor exhibition hall. Photos: courtesy Kure Maritime Museum/Yamato Museum.

**National WWI Museum and Memorial Exhibits, Historic Liberty Memorial, Kansas City, Missouri, USA, 2006**
ASAI Architecture; exhibition design: Ralph Appelbaum Associates

As discussed within this book's introduction, the interwar years witnessed the creation of several museum buildings that commemorated World War I. This museum in Kansas City was dedicated on Armistice day, November 11, 1926 as the Liberty Memorial, with a museum within that showcased their artifacts acquired after 1920. Harold Van Buren Magonigle was its architect, one often associated with commemorative monuments in the United States such as the McKinley Memorial (1907) in Canton, Ohio, and the U.S.S. *Maine* monument (1913) in Columbus Circle, midtown Manhattan, New York City. Magonigle's design for the Liberty Memorial was won in competition, its funding led by prominent Kansas City industrialists and philanthropists who also raised more than $ 2.5 million for the construction in 1919. Groundbreaking took place in 1921 with the dedication in five years. The limestone complex designed in an overall nod to Egyptian Revival style includes the Liberty memorial tower 265 feet (81 m) high flanked by Exhibition and Memory halls. Stone Assyrian sphynxes flanking the tower cover their faces with their wings. The tower itself had an artificially lit top which featured steam colored by lights. The grounds were designed by George Kessler, a Kansas City landscape architect who also designed the city's park system and was one of the key players in initially spearheading this memorial.

In the early 1980s, exhibits within were refreshed but the major boost to those visitor experiences and restoration and expansion of the building came in the early 2000s. The memorial raised over $ 100 million towards restoration, renovation and an 80,000 square feet (7432 sq. m) underground expansion. Congress designated the memorial as the nation's official World War I museum in 2004, this being further being reinforced by President Barack Obama in 2014 with the designation National World War I Museum and Memorial. Much of the credit for this goes to exhibit designer Ralph Appelbaum, praised for his firm's work on the exhibitions within the National Holocaust Museum in Washington, D.C. Appelbaum created an important exhibition within this Kansas City museum, opening to the public in 2006, being praised by scholars, critics and the general public alike. His design incorporated a variety of themed spaces preceded by a theatrical presentation held within a space that included a life-size tableau of »No-Man's Land«. Other full-scale features include a trench as well as an enormous bomb crater to immerse visitors in the experience. The most talked about feature, however, is the glass entry bridge under which over 9,000 poppies represent the nine million combatants killed in the war. The museum also includes visitor amenities such as a museum store and »Over There« café, and an important research center for historians. Since the 2006 reopening the museum has continued to improve facilities, including 2013 restoration of the artificial flame atop the tower and inclusion of a changing exhibitions gallery. The museum sees over 300,000 visitors annually.

1. Museum exterior in the plaza.
2. Exhibit hall.
3. Paul Sunderland Glass Bridge and poppy field.
All photos: National World War I Museum and Memorial.

AUGUST
SEPTEMBER
OCTOBER
NOVEMBER
DECEMBER
1915

4. »Chronology of World War I« exhibition.
5. »No Man's Land« as part of the Horizon Theater.
Photos: National World War I Museum and Memorial.

**National Museum of the Marine Corps, Triangle, Virginia, USA, 2006**
Fentress-Bradburn Architects; exhibition design: Christopher Chadbourne & Associates

When anyone is asked about an iconic image of the United States Marine Corps, they usually cite the Marine Corps Memorial sculpture by Felix De Weldon or its source of inspiration, the Joe Rosenthal photo, both showing the raising of the American Flag on Mt. Suribachi during the Battle of Iwo Jima (1945). Adaptations of the image were used for the Seventh War Bond Drive which raised $ 24 billion for the war effort in spring-summer 1945. Over a million posters were shown in theaters, banks, shop windows, and railroad stations, and enlarged on billboards, all across the nation. With that legendary image in mind, it is no wonder that Curt Fentress was selected from a competition to design the museum, initiated 1999 and funded by the Marine Corps as well as the Marine Corps Heritage Foundation.

Fentress, known mostly for his airport terminals in Denver, Los Angeles, and Inchon South Korea, has also done museums such as the National Museum of Wildlife Art (1995) and he is currently designing the National Museum of Intelligence and Special Operations. His design for the Marine Corps Museum draws on the angular composition of the famed Rosenthal photograph for the ten-story, 210 feet (64 m) high steel and glass tower. This caps the atrium lobby »Leatherneck Gallery« of the museum. The angular spire becomes a highly visible landmark from Interstate 95 nearby. It also acts in airflow exhaust. Much of the 110,000 square feet (10,219 sq. m) building is constructed into the 135 acres (55 ha) site, with a large portion beyond the spire under a green roof. Galleries, offices and visitor services radiate around that central organizing space. Christopher Chadbourne & Associates designed most of the exhibitions and Studio Eis created the life cast mannequins, particularly striking within the central »Leatherneck Gallery«. Galleries were added to the core in 2010, and the final phase of gallery and theater construction is taking place now, targeted for a 2020 completion. Initial total cost of the building was approximately $ 490 million paid by a public-private partnership between the Marine Corps and the Marine Corps Heritage Foundation. The former supported the design and exhibits totaling a third of that, the other two-thirds being slated for foundation-supported construction costs. The Marine Corps itself supports the maintenance and management of the building.

Fentress created a master plan for museum expansion as well as other facilities nearby. This includes a parade ground, memorial garden and park, rifle range, and a gem of a seventy-seven seat chapel (2009). The 2,100 square feet (195 sq. m) contemplative space, built of Douglas fir timber and stone, was donated by former Marine Captain Timothy Day who founded Bar-S Foods Co. in Phoenix.

In all, Fentress has designed a distinctive museum building and campus for the Marine Corps. Despite its essentially ex-urban location, it accommodates more than 500,000 visitors each year.

1. Aerial view. Photo: Marine Corps Heritage Foundation, courtesy Fentress Architects.
2. Central Leatherneck Gallery showing suspended Vought Corsairs and other aircraft. Photo: © Astula Inc., Raul Garcia.
3. C. C.Beal, *7th War Loan – Now-all Together*, after Associated Press photo for the U.S. Department of the Treasury. U.S. Government Printing Office, 1945. Photo: Library of Congress, Prints and Photographs Division.
4. Main-level plan. Photo: © Fentress Architects.

7th WAR LOAN NOW··ALL TOGETHER


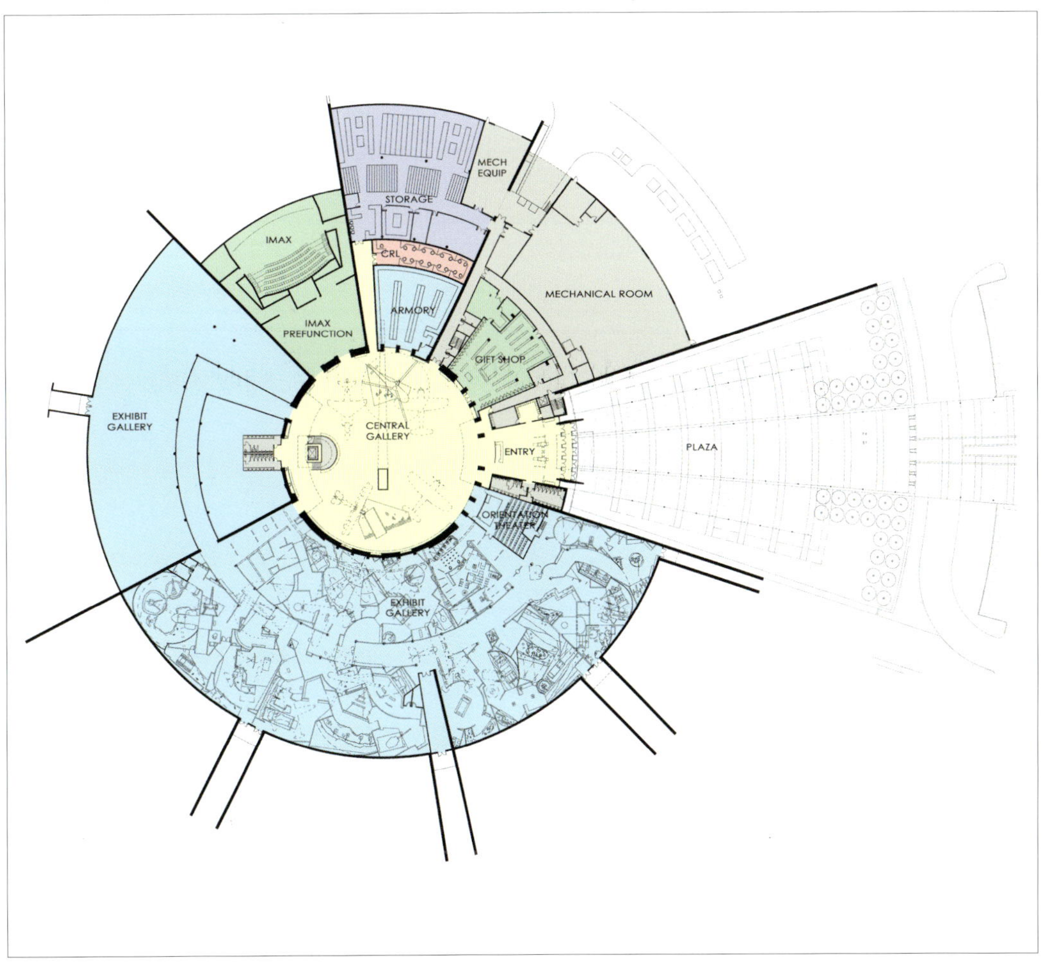

STORAGE
MECH EQUIP
IMAX
CRL
MECHANICAL ROOM
ARMORY
IMAX PREFUNCTION
GIFT SHOP
EXHIBIT GALLERY
CENTRAL GALLERY
ENTRY
PLAZA
ORIENTATION THEATER
EXHIBIT GALLERY

5. Chapel exterior. Photo: © Jason A. Knowles.
6. Chapel interior: Photo: © Astula Inc., Raul Garcia.
7. Chapel site plan. Photo: © Fentress Architects.

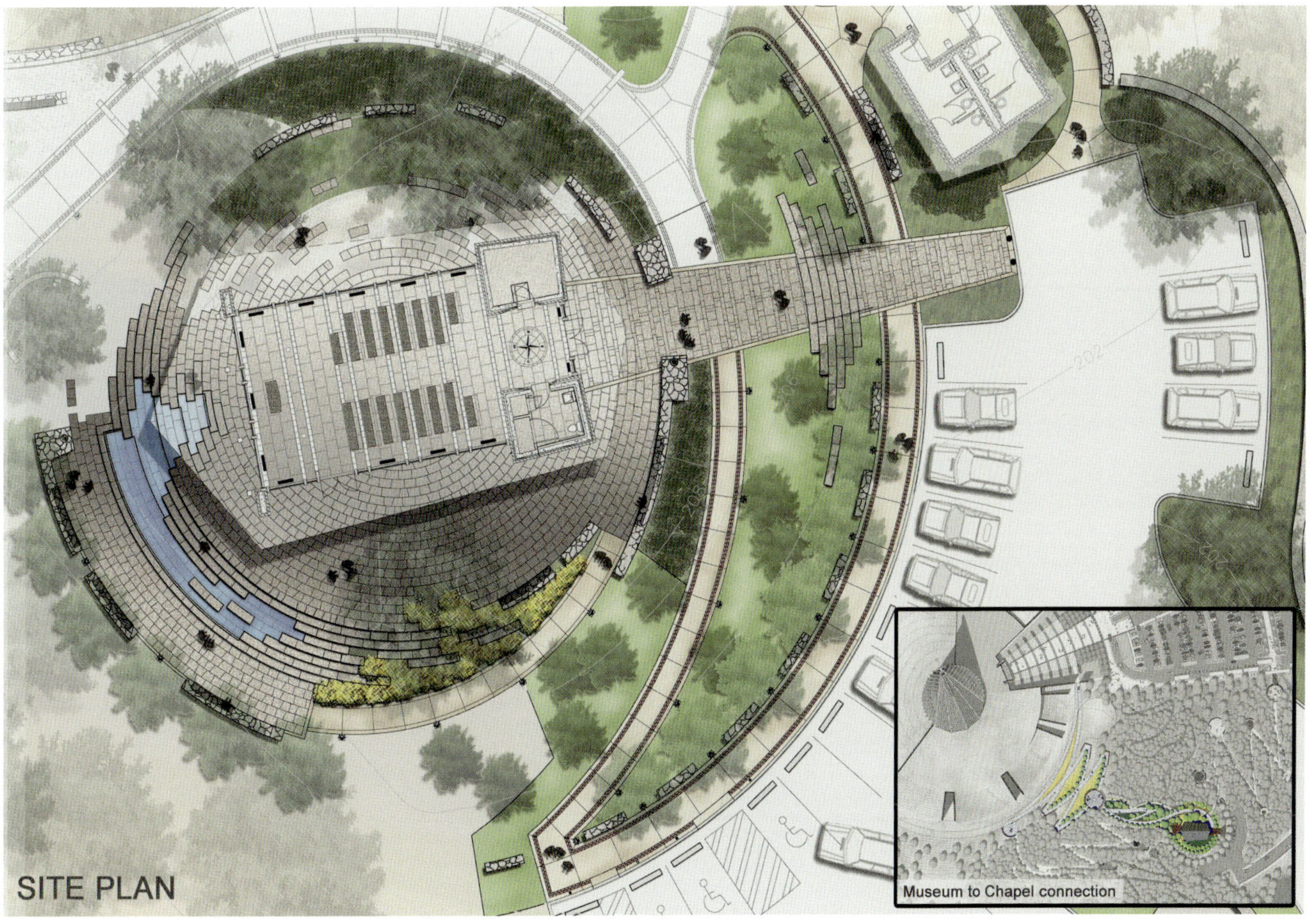

**Puget Sound Navy Museum, Bremerton, Washington, USA, 2007**
Korte Company, with Synergy Construction

**National Museum of the American Sailor, Great Lakes Naval Station, North Chicago, Illinois, USA, 2006**
Vinci Hamp Architects

The United States Navy operates a headquarters museum at the Naval Yard in Washington, D.C., as well as nine other officially-sanctioned Navy museums across the country. The offsite partner museums are government supported but also rely on private foundation donations. The ten museums in total are managed by the Naval History & Heritage Command. Two of these are particularly interesting as regards their architectural stories, and preservation issues today.

The earliest of these is Building 50, now the Puget Sound Navy Museum. The 1895/96 wood Classicist building was constructed for $ 7,900 to be the first administrative headquarters for the Puget Sound Naval Shipyard & Intermediate Maintenance Facility (PSNS & IMF) on Sinclair Inlet. It was originally designed by Seattle architects Chamberlin and Siebrand. A 1903 addition was built at the rear. What is amazing about this building is the resilience of its wooden structure. It has been moved three times in its history to accommodate new construction projects. The first was when Dry Dock 2 was built in 1910 where the building was moved west. In 1939 it was moved again to another location because of Dry Dock 5 construction. Finally, in 2004, Building 50 was moved off the shipyard grounds to a publicly accessible location on Bremerton's waterfront. In its lifetime, the building served as the offices of shipyard commanders, a chemistry lab, apprentice school, dispensary, and now, in its final move, a museum.

Although some of its decorative elements have been removed, most remain and have been restored, including its paint after the original scheme. Opening in 2007, the museum building was donated to the City of Bremerton by the Navy. It has approximately 8,000 square feet (743 sq. m) of exhibition space. A double-storey steel and glass Modernist addition at the rear offers entertaining space for receptions on Bremerton's waterfront. Before moving here, the Puget Sound Navy Museum was founded 1954 and was situated in several locations. Its exhibits and collections focus on the shipyard history and the Navy, along with having travelling exhibits as well. Its 70,000 visitors annually get to see those artifacts as well as the submarine sail in the entry plaza, dedicated to the U.S.S. *Parche*, decommissioned 2004.

By contrast with engineering the move of a vintage frame building, the next preservation story involves another wood-frame structure on a Navy base, some 2,000 miles (3,218 km) east at Naval Station Great Lakes, 35 miles (56.32 km) north of Chicago on Lake Michigan. Naval Station Great Lakes is an important facility that serves as the home of the Navy's only boot camp and other important apprentice-level training for Enlisted Sailors. Chicago-based architect Jarvis Hunt designed the base, which was officially dedicated on October 28, 1911. The base grew tremendously over the years, most notably during World War II. Architect Gordon Bunshaft of the prominent firm Skidmore, Owings & Merrill designed Building 42, the Hostess House, in 1942. Like many wartime constructions, this one-and-a half storey, 23,000 sq. feet (2136.76 sq. m) timber facility was constructed of non-strategic materials. It is located directly north of the installation's main gate on Farragut Avenue off Main Street. During World War II, the facility served as a welcome center for 969,000 sailors who trained at the base.

In 2006, Chicago architects Vinci Hamp restored the building's north façade to its original appearance. In 2008, Building 42 became the official home of the Great Lakes Naval Museum. In 2009, the museum became an official Department of the Navy museum operated by the Naval History & Heritage Command. In 2014, the Secretary of the Navy approved the renaming of the Great Lakes Naval Museum as the National Museum of the American Sailor. The museum, which sees 50,000 visitors annually, is the only official Navy museum dedicated to collecting, preserving, and educating the public about the history of the American Enlisted Sailor and how their dedication and sacrifice has been instrumental to the fleet's success. In July 2017, the National Museum of the American Sailor Foundation proposed additional gallery space in a commercial development adjacent to Naval Station Great Lakes, yet to be constructed, which would serve as a supplemental museum facility to Building 42, the Hostess House.

Puget Sound Navy Museum, Bremerton

1. U.S.S. *Parche* final voyage in 2004. Photo: National Archives.
2. Building 50 move in October 1910. Photo: Puget Sound Navy Museum.
3. Building 50 move in 2004. Photo: U.S. Navy, courtesy the Korte Company.
4. Sail from former U.S.S. *Parche* and current Building 50 in the background. Photo: Puget Sound Navy Museum.

National Museum of the American Sailor, Great Lakes Naval Station, North Chicago

1, 2. Building 42, Exteriors from the southeast and southwest in 1942. Photos: Chicago History Museum, Hedrich Blessing Collection, HB-07226-E and F.
3. Exterior from the northwest in 2017. Photo: author.

**Visitor Center, American Cemetery, Colleville-sur-Mer, Normandy, France. 2007**
Smith Group JJR, Architects; exhibition design: Gallagher & Associates

The American Battle Monuments Commission-ABMC was founded 1923, to commemorate the armed forces where they have served since 1917, establish appropriate war memorials and burial grounds in foreign countries, control the design of such monuments, and encourage sponsorship for their maintenance. There are twenty-six cemeteries and twenty-nine memorials under their care. Their cemeteries and monuments memorialize 140,000 service personnel who have died and the more than 94,000 missing in action. They employ 422 people and have an annual budget of $ 75 million. One site within their care is the American Cemetery and Memorial in Normandy at Colleville-sur-Mer, established June 8, 1944, two days after D-day. It is one of two American cemeteries in Normandy; there are a total of twenty-four of them for the many thousands of Allied and German troops who fought and died here.

In this one at Colleville-sur-Mer, 9,387 are buried. The 172 acres (69.6 ha) cemetery overlooks Omaha Beach, one of five landing points during D-Day. The cemetery and memorial colonnades were planned by Harbeson, Hough, Livingston & Larson, Markley Stevenson, and sculptor Donald De Lue. Just east of the cemetery is the new visitor center designed by the Smith Group JJR.

The architects, with locations across the United States and China, have done museum design work for the Cranbrook Art Museum, Detroit Institute of Arts, National Museum of the American Indian, National Museum of African American History and Culture, and the White House Visitor Center. They designed this Normandy building with associate architect John Lampros from Paris, with landscaping by Michael Vergason Landscape Architects, and D. Paysage from Paris. A goal of the design was not to compete with the cemetery but to create a building that was compatible with the landscape and historic topic yet distinct from the cemetery's architecture. The Modernist granite clad, steel frame building of 30,000 square feet (2,787 sq. m) evokes the rough terrain in a very minimalist way, having an architectural dialogue with the 20 acres (8 ha) site as well as with the English Channel and Omaha Beach below. Interiors use concrete, limestone and wood.

Exhibits within were designed by Gallagher & Associates, a firm founded by Patrick Gallagher that, for more than three decades, specializes in museum experiences. The contract here was part of a larger body of work they have done for the ABMC for a variety of sites in Europe and Hawaii. Here, their exhibit work is mostly underground within the pavilion, the approximately 10,000 square feet (929 sq. m) space evocative of bunkers.

Three themes of Competence, Courage, and Sacrifice organize the installation which has both static and immersive aspects. These range from panels through artifacts and media, the focus of which relates to personal connections of individual stories by those who fought and died here. A corridor in which visitors hear a recitation of the name of every individual buried in the cemetery leads visitors to the final area – Sacrifice. After seeing the exhibition, visitors leave the building on a walkway directing them to the cemetery. The new visitor center, budgeted at $ 30 million, is an important interpretive and contemplative addition to the American cemetery here.

1. Exterior. Photo: © Roland Halbe.
2. Interior looking towards the English Channel. Photo: © Roland Halbe.
3, 4. Exhibit panels, cases and theater. Photos: Guillaume Murat courtesy Gallagher & Associates.

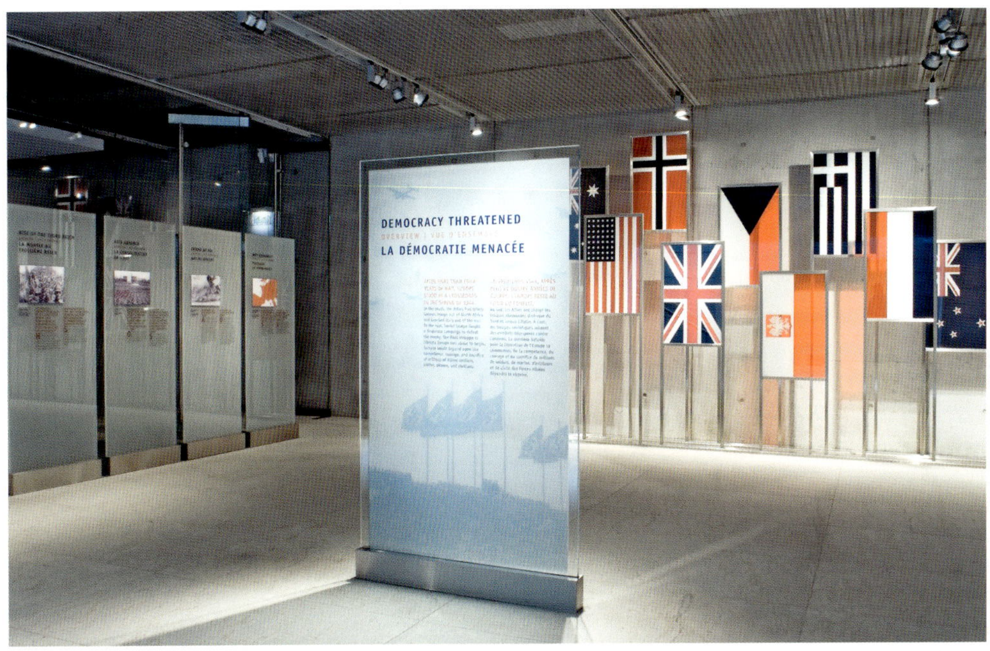
DEMOCRACY THREATENED
LA DÉMOCRATIE MENACÉE

OBSTACLES AND CONCERNS
OBSTACLES ET INQUIÉTUDES
EXPERIENCE AND VISION
EXPÉRIENCE ET PRÉVISION

**Royal Air Force National Cold War Exhibition, Cosford, England, 2007**
Feilden, Clegg and Bradley Studios; exhibition design: Neal Potter Design Associates

The Royal Air Force/RAF commemorates its centennial in 2018, being founded April 1, 1918 from the Royal Flying Corps and the Royal Naval Air Service. Its first museum opened 1972 at the former RAF base at Colindale-Hendon, now within London. The site is going through a master plan and additions discussed later in this volume (see p. 118). Their next museum site was developed 1979 at the RAF base of Cosford, about 30 miles (48 km) northwest of Birmingham. The base is still an active training and educational one for the RAF, including a basic flight training Volunteer Reserve unit associated with the University of Birmingham and other local schools. The museum there grew, additional aircraft requiring a number of new buildings just northwest of the base's runway, constructed 1998 through 2002. Today their visitorship exceeds 350,000 each year. Architecturally, the most interesting of these buildings is the one housing the Cold War Exhibition.

Architects Feilden, Clegg and Bradley have been in practice for more than four decades, its current senior partners being Peter Clegg and Keith Bradley. Recent cultural works include renovation of the Southbank Centre (2018), the Royal Birmingham Conservatoire (2017), University of Roehampton Library (2017) and the Manchester School of Art (2013). Their award-winning National Cold War Exhibition (2007) is a dynamic, jet-age, enclosure housing nineteen aircraft, along with various vehicles and memorabilia. These are interpreted through multimedia hotspots or audio-visual pods created by designer Neal Potter. Those have themes such as The Berlin Airlift, Cuban Missile Crisis, and Space Race.

The building was engineered by the Michael Bradley Partnership and SH structures Ltd., its spine being 82 feet high x 443 feet long (25x135 m), the resulting plan articulated with a bolted tubular steel structure. The aluminum clad exterior is seen as two opposite twisting or warped triangular forms, making a dynamically curved building. The idea behind this was to visually illustrate the two opposing forces in the Cold War – east and west, Warsaw Pact and NATO/North Atlantic Treaty Organization. Interior museum space is tempered using controlled ventilation and conservation heat sources, eliminating the need for high energy air conditioning. A demountable fabric wall on one end provides access to remove aircraft. The upper level contains a viewing bridge whereas the lower level also has classrooms and an auditorium. The total space is 86,111 square feet (8,000 sq. m) with construction costs being some £ 9 million, and all total costs at £ 12.5 million. The eight aircraft suspended at various points from the structure provide visitors with a dramatic display and a challenge for conservators. Each year, a team hired from Total Access dusts the airplanes and inspects the rigging, team workers themselves suspended from the ceiling.

1. South view. Photo: Tim Burton SH Structures.
2. Aerial view. Photo: Van Rhijn Aerial Photography.

pp. 56, 57
3–5. Interiors showing various aircraft rigged from the steel roof trusses, including Hawker Hunter and English Electric/BAE Lightning. Photos: Tim Burton SH Structures.

MELTING THE
COLD
WAR
XG337
THE SINATRA DOCTRINE
"MY WAY"
COLLAPSE
OF COMMUNISM
REFORMS

**Flying Heritage Collection, now Flying Heritage & Combat Armor Museum, Paine Field, Everett, Washington, USA. Restoration of historic hangar space, 2008**
Owen Richards Architects

Microsoft co-founder Paul Allen has developed museums before, perhaps the most famous of these being the Frank Gehry-designed Experience Music Project (2000) in Seattle, created with Jody Allen, his sister. It was based on the Jimmy Hendrix collection and Seattle's influence on Rock and Roll. A science fiction component was added 2004 and the entire museum rebranded 2013 as the EMP. Although Allen and his sister originally focused on interactivity and visitor participation, in some ways that idea expanded to his creation of the Flying Heritage Collection at Paine Field, north of Seattle at Everett, Washington. Seattle already had a great aerospace museum collection with the Museum of Flight and its static display of historic aircraft. The Flying Heritage Collection takes it a step further in that almost all of their historic aircraft are operable. Allen has funded major salvage and restoration operations for some of these, including very rare aircraft such as a Russian Ilyushin IL-2 Stumovik attack bomber and Japanese Ki-43 Oscar fighter. He also has expanded his collection to military vehicles, some rare ones being a German Hetzer tank destroyer and Japanese Type 95 Ha-Go tank. He started collecting historic planes in 1998 and opened his museum 2004, moving it to its current location 2008 after this historic hangar was restored 2007/08.

Architect Owen Richards graduated from Rice University and worked in architectural firms in Atlanta, New York, and Seattle before starting his own firm in 2004. He has designed both museums as well as aviation buildings. Here, he restored a 53,000 square feet (4,924 sq. m) hangar for twenty of those aircraft, providing museum entry, store and office space as well. The interiors were stripped of later intrusions and the spaces and structure painted white to visually unify the open space. The concrete floor was stripped of its paint and ground and polished, and the 1930s apron airside was also refinished. The exterior's original corrugated siding of 1949 was restored and incompatible materials removed. Corrugated plastic skylights were replaced with ultraviolet polycarbonate glazing. When initially opened in June 2008, it received more than 20,000 visitors in the first four months of operation.

Since this initial restoration, the Flying Heritage Collection has expanded to twenty-six aircraft and also twenty-five military vehicles, exhibited in over 75,000 square feet (6,968 sq. m) by adding a new building of 22,000 square feet (2,044 sq. m) in 2013. Hangar 3 is another one newly opened in 2018 that adds some 30,000 square feet (2,787 sq. m) of space since the museum now incorporates both aircraft and vehicles such as tanks. Accordingly, its name and branding have changed 2017 to the Flying Heritage & Combat Armor Museum. The museum hosts both summer airshows as well as tank demonstrations. New permanent interactive exhibits include »Why War: The Causes of Conflict«. Allen himself continues to fund underwater expeditions, the most recent being the 2017 discovery of the cruiser U.S.S. *Indianapolis* in the Philippine Sea sunk 1945, and the 2018 discovery of the U.S.S. *Lexington*, an aircraft carrier sunk in the Coral Sea, 1942.

1–3. Exterior and interiors of restored hangar, including aircraft such as a P-47D and P-51D. Photos: © Benjamin Benschneider.

PROXIMIT
FUSE
1944
UPUPA EPOPS

**Intrepid Sea, Air & Space Museum, New York, New York, USA, 2008**
Exhibition design and pier reconstruction: Perkins + Will and Dattner Architects

New York real estate developer Zachary Fisher and his family spearheaded a series of foundations and funds to support veterans and military families, these existing today as the Fallen Heroes Fund, the Fisher House Foundation, and the Intrepid Museum Foundation. The museum is centered on the former U.S.S. *Intrepid*, one of twenty-four Essex Class aircraft carriers built in World War II. It is also one of four Essex class aircraft carrier museums, the others being in Charleston, South Carolina (*Yorktown*), Oakland, California (*Hornet*), and Corpus Christi, Texas (*Lexington*).

The Intrepid opened 1982 at Pier 86, off Manhattan's 46th Street and the Hudson River. The museum complex had grown over the years to include a decommissioned early nuclear missile submarine U.S.S. *Growler* (1989), numerous jet age aircraft including an A-12 Blackbird, foreign planes such as an Israeli Kfir and Polish MiG21, and a record-setting British Airways Concorde G-BOAD (2003). More recent acquisitions (2011/12) include space age artifacts such as a Soyuz TMA-6 re-entry capsule and OV-101 *Enterprise*, the first test space shuttle. Both the Soyuz and shuttle are exhibited within a temporary pavilion on the flight deck. With major objects representing sea, air and space, the museum utilizes the history of the ship and its crew to teach a variety of family friendly programs and educational efforts focused on Science, Technology, Engineering, and Math/STEM, reaching over 1 million people a year. The book *Interpreting Naval History* praises the museum's innovative best practices to expand the audience (see selected sources at the end of this volume).

In 2006 the orignal Pier 86 was in need of replacement. As part of a more than $ 115 million project completed 2008, the *Intrepid* and *Growler* were drydocked and the Concorde removed while the pier was being rebuilt to the designs of Dattner Architects. Dattner also redid some of the historic spaces on the ship, particularly those forward in the forecastle (fo'c'sle).

After an invited competition, Ralph Johnson and Eva Maddox of Perkins + Will were selected to redesign the hangar deck exhibition as well as create a style guide for all exhibition components that might be added in the future. Their design focused on a media-wall entry and information desk, and then a more than 200 feet (60.96 m) long steel and glass display case that represented a timeline of the *Intrepid's* history from 1943 to 1974. The display case is within hangars one and two. The two sides of this dramatic case hold objects and interactives related to the ship's functioning and the sailors and aviators who served aboard, the »humanity behind the hardware«. They also designed a wall midway through the exhibition synchronized with a multi-media program on the kamikaze attack of November 25, 1944, paying tribute to all those lost in *Intrepid* combat.

After visitors explore this museum zone they approach a large open space of approximately 10,000 square feet (929 sq. m) in hangar three towards the aft end of the ship, with a series of interactives for families and children. The space is called the »Exploreum«. Most of these interactives can be moved to the perimeter to accommodate any number of corporate events. The museum holds many of these as well as exhibits throughout its facilities such as the pier, flight deck, and Michael Tyler Fisher Center for Education at the aft end of the ship.

1. Aerial view of the Hudson River, showing the Intrepid Museum at Pier 86. Photo: Pisa Photography, shutterstock.com.
2. *Intrepid* from embankment showing temporary space shuttle pavilion aft. Photo: shutterstock.com.
3. Axonometric cutaway, 2007. The view shows the entry point opposite the media wall top right and »Exploreum« interactive zone bottom left. Photo: courtesy Perkins + Will, © Intrepid Sea, Air & Space Museum.
4. Memorial Wall and TBM Avenger. Photo: Jon Miller of Hedrich Blessing, © Intrepid Sea, Air & Space Museum.

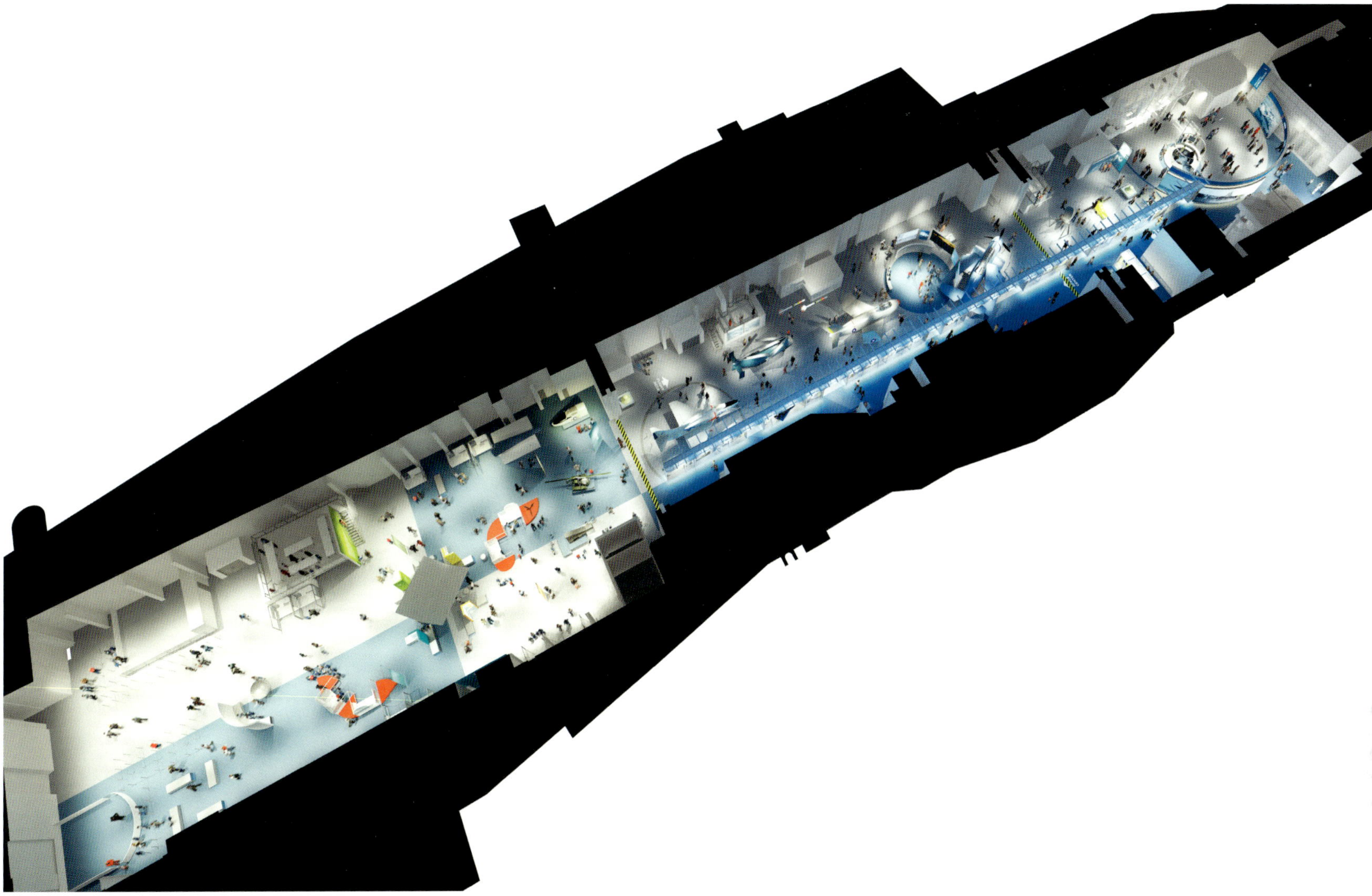

pp. 62, 63
5. Exhibition on the hangar deck, as built 2008 with TBM Avenger, FJ3 Fury, and A4B Skyhawk. Photo: Jon Miller of Hedrich Blessing, © Intrepid Sea, Air & Space Museum.
6. Space Shuttle *Enterprise* within its temporary exhibit pavilion on the flight deck, 2013. Photo: © Mark Greenberg.
7. »Exploreum« interactive family zone. Photo: author.
8. Salute to Freedom dinner setup in Exploreum, 2018. Photo: © Carlos Varela Photography.

AF
203

Enterprise
United States

**Gettysburg National Military Park Museum & Visitor Center, Gettysburg, Pennsylvania, USA, 2009**

LSC Design (today Warehaus); exhibition design: Gallagher & Associates

Just about every American knows that the Gettysburg Address on November 19, 1863 by President Abraham Lincoln proclaimed the Civil War (1861 to 1865) as a struggle for freedom and equality for all. He noted the dedication of a national cemetery here to honor those Union soldiers who died in this battle more than four months before, when their armies defeated Confederate ones. The actual battle of July 1–3, 1863 marked the northernmost advance of Confederate forces which, after the Union victory, were essentially in retreat over the next two years. The battle involved more than 180,000 soldiers from both sides with 51,000 casualties, and there are monuments to both armies and leaders throughout the area. The battlefield is arguably one of the most important pilgrimage sites for military buffs and the general public alike. More than a million people each year visit the park as well as the new visitor center.

The park had a smaller, earlier visitor center (see p. 10, introduction) that was replaced by this current one of 140,000 square feet (13,006 sq. m) at a total architectural cost of $ 29.4 million. The Gettysburg National Military Park Museum & Visitor Center, a partnership between the National Park Service and the Gettysburg Foundation, is arguably one of the largest and most successful public-private partnerships of its kind in the United States. The architects designed a masonry and steel-frame structure with contextual references to rural buildings, more commonly made of masonry and wood. The new museum's master plan, developed in conjunction with the Gettysburg Foundation, helped to redefine the National Park Service's model for museums and visitor centers guaranteeing the preservation of the nation's largest collection of some civil war artifacts and conveying the events surrounding this pivotal moment in history. The museum exhibits by Gallagher & Associates display these objects within 20,000 square feet (1,858 sq. m) of space. The most important exhibit feature, however, is the famed 1884 variant Cyclorama panoramic painting of Pickett's Charge by Paul Dominique Phillipoteaux, the largest oil painting in North America at 377 feet wide by 42 feet tall (114.9 x 12.8 m). One of the largest art restoration projects in America; twenty-eight specialists worked over two years to preserve this artwork. Construction had to be phased in order to create a working, controlled museum environment large enough to accommodate the Cyclorama. The destination also showcases two state of the art theaters, a »Refreshment Saloon«-restaurant, bookstore and nearby tours of the battlefield.

Perhaps equally significant, the building was designed to meet Leadership in Energy and Environmental Design/LEED performance certification standards and was awarded Gold Level Certification in 2010. This involved a variety of aspects from geothermal heating and cooling to utilizing recycled wood from a nearby barn. This is especially significant given the typical energy consumption of museum facilities due to exacting standards – including lighting, temperature, and humidity, required for preservation. In this way, the building not only preserves our history but also serves as a steward of our future.

1. Aerial view. The stone-clad building in the center marks the entry, with the museum and Cyclorama building at the right and the »Refreshment Saloon« at the far left.
2, 3. Cyclorama painting and museum display.
Photos: © warehausae.com.

"Now we are engaged in … il war…"
The Gettysburg Museum
… THE AMERICAN CIVIL WAR

**National Infantry Museum, Fort Benning, Georgia, USA, 2009**
Verner Johnson Inc.; exhibition design: Christopher Chadbourne & Associates

Fort Benning was established 1918 next to the City of Columbus, Georgia, during World War I as a school to train infantrymen. More permanent buildings were constructed 1922 through the 1930s, and the name changed from Camp Benning to Fort Benning – the name commemorates Confederate Brigadier General Henry L. Benning. Vintage postcards can be seen on eBay today showing the Baroque-Classicist Old Infantry School from the interwar years. This domed building, in a way, served as a source of inspiration and counterpoint to the domed, Classicist National Infantry Museum just to the west of the base, and east of the open space of the Oxbow Meadows Environmental Park and Oxbow Creek Golf Course. The museum is oriented north and south, with the domed entry and parking lot on the north. The Boston architectural firm of Verner Johnson Inc. specializes in museums, such as the redesign of the Cincinnati Museum Center (1990), expansion of the Great Lakes Science Center (1996) in Cleveland, to the more recent Flint Hills Discovery Center (2012) in Manhattan, Kansas and Tubman African American Museum (2015) in Macon, Georgia.

The firm's work at the National Infantry Museum was directed by their head architect Brad Nederhoff. He presented a formal building on the 200 acres (80.94 ha) site within a formal visitor progression as they approach the building. The building was spearheaded by Major General Jerry White and the National Infantry Museum Foundation. The entire museum has 190,000 square feet (17,651 sq. m) of space and the overall cost was $ 100 million. It was intended as a home for the collection of 300,000 artifacts as well as a memorial to all infantrymen. The domed entry housing the *Follow Me* statue of a soldier suggests monumentality of classical buildings and its lightness of architectural forms suggests openness, something that the museum's foundation liked regarding both aspects.

Visitors enter the building and proceed longitudinally towards the south. Highlights within include »The Last 100 Yards« series of theatrical vignettes created by the exhibition design firm, Christopher Chadbourne & Associates, with life cast mannequins by Studio Eis. The architect and museum foundation focused on high quality materials for public spaces, such as granite, terrazzo and cherry wood. Red Georgia brick was used on the exterior. Interior exhibition spaces contain interactives, an IMAX 3D theater, education space, as well as offices and visitor amenities such as a museum store and »Fife & Drum« restaurant and bar. The museum grounds contain a Vietnam Memorial Plaza and a Global War on Terrorism Memorial. And of particular architectural interest are the World War II era reconstructed wood frame barracks, mess hall, orderly room, supply room, chapel, and sleeping quarters and headquarters of General George S. Patton, all salvaged from the nearby base. The overall museum experience inside and out was designed to accommodate an annual visitorship of 500,000. Since opening the museum has had more than two million visitors.

1. Aerial view. Photo: Harlan Hambright, courtesy Verner Johnson Inc.
2. Site plan. Photo: courtesy Verner Johnson Inc.
3, 4. »The Last 100 Yards« Gallery: 1862 and 1918. Photos: Harlan Hambright, courtesy Verner Johnson Inc.

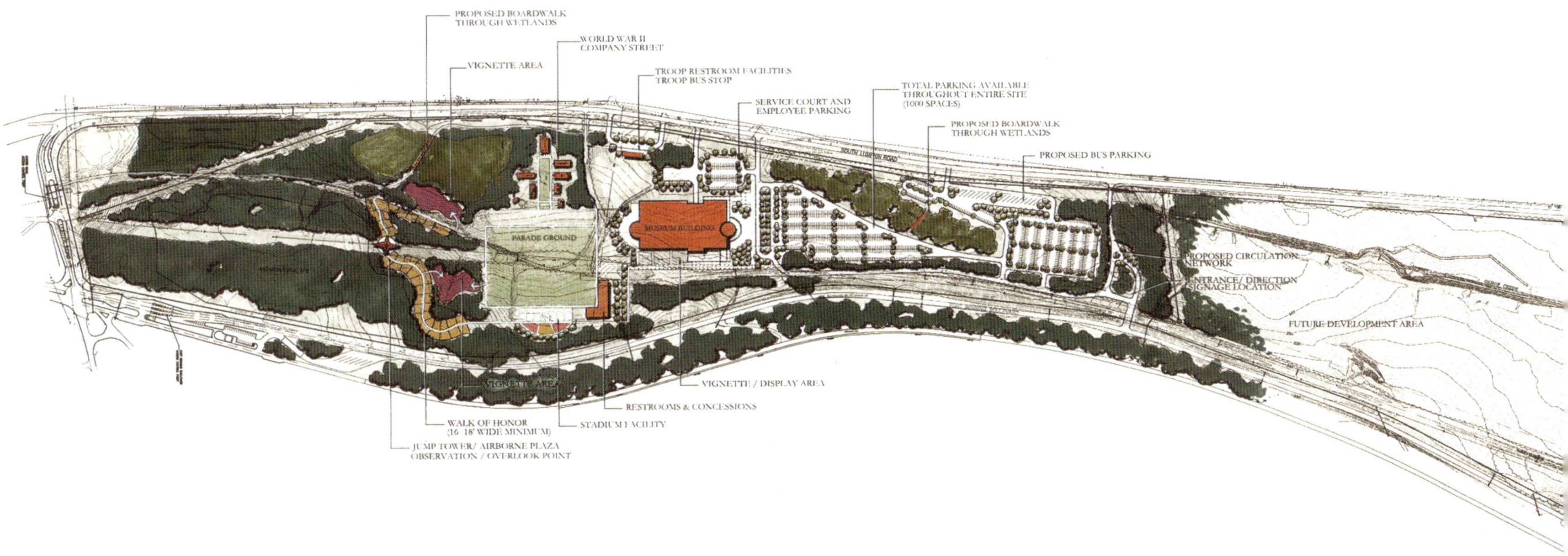
PROPOSED BOARDWALK
THROUGH WETLANDS
WORLD WAR II
COMPANY STREET
VIGNETTE AREA
TROOP RESTROOM FACILITIES
TROOP BUS STOP
TOTAL PARKING AVAILABLE
THROUGHOUT ENTIRE SITE
(1000 SPACES)
SERVICE COURT AND
EMPLOYEE PARKING
PROPOSED BOARDWALK
THROUGH WETLANDS
PROPOSED BUS PARKING
MUSEUM BUILDING
PARADE GROUND
PROPOSED CIRCULATION
NETWORK
ENTRANCE/ DIRECTION
SIGNAGE LOCATION
FUTURE DEVELOPMENT AREA
VIGNETTE AREA
VIGNETTE / DISPLAY AREA
RESTROOMS & CONCESSIONS
WALK OF HONOR
(16'-18' WIDE MINIMUM)
STADIUM FACILITY
JUMP TOWER/ AIRBORNE PLAZA
OBSERVATION / OVERLOOK POINT

ANTIETAM

**The Tank Museum, Bovington, England, 2009**
Kennedy O'Callaghan Architects with Terence O'Rourke; exhibition design: PLB Projects Ltd.

The Tank Museum is an amazing institution. Situated in Dorset in southwest England, it is an extension of the Royal Tank Regiment/Royal Armored Corps. The museum focuses on the history of armored vehicles from World War I through the present. Its location in Bovington is a historic one that can be traced back to the 1916 tank training facility there. The museum itself was established 1923. It is the world's largest collection of such vehicles with 300 of them. More than a traditional museum of static display, a number of these are operable and used in educational programs, displays, and their annual Tankfest. Although collecting and exhibiting tanks back decades, the museum received an enormous boost in its displays and architecture with the master plan and building designed by London-based Kennedy O'Callaghan Architects. This practice was established in 1998, focusing on conservation and museums, particularly those that are Heritage Lottery Fund/HLF funded. Some of their work related to military museums includes conservation planning for the Royal Air Force Museum's historic buildings at Hendon as well as conservation of historic buildings at Bletchley Park (see p. 76). Their major design in this field has been the Tank Museum.

Their building consists of a display of important tanks from the twentieth century within a pie-shaped, quarter-circle exhibition hall of concrete, steel and glass of more than 47,361 square feet (4,400 sq. m), having overhead north-facing natural lighting. The building is cut into the landscape which slopes to the south. The entry space at the upper level has a café and soft-play area for kids. That level connects to the main hall with concrete ramps that also act as viewing platforms. The mezzanine also contains an indoor picnic area while the grass bank outside the performance arena is also used for that. Exhibits were redone 2014, and additional exhibit, education, and restoration workshop spaces are adjacent. Tanks include *Little Willie* (1915), prototype for the world's first tank, to a functioning Tiger I tank captured in Tunisia (1943), and the more current British Challenger 2.

The building's low, ground hugging form was inspired by current tank profiles and the shed-like exhibit interiors are akin to hangar spaces in many other military museums, particularly aviation ones. A glazed and aluminum clad control tower 82 feet (25 m) high allows the curators to orchestrate and narrate Tankfest and other active displays below in the arena. The entire project cost £ 16 million with £ 9.6 million coming from an HLF grant. Despite being situated where some may think isolated, the museum draws over 200,000 visitors annually.

1. Aerial view showing the museum complex, including control tower and landscaped area lower left, for Tankfest action programs. Photo: courtesy Kennedy O'Callaghan Architects.
2. Exterior with control tower and Challenger 2 tank. Photo: shutterstock.com.
3,4. Main exhibit hall and ramp. Photos: The Tank Museum UK.

**Pritzker Military Museum & Library, Monroe Building, Chicago, Illinois, USA, 2010**
Holabird & Root and TVS Design

Colonel (IL) Jennifer N. Pritzker, IL ARNG (retired) founded this institution in 2003. She has a strong interest in both military history and the preservation of historic architecture. The library and its exhibits and programs broadcast across the Chicagoland area were headquartered in rented space within a commercial building that was once the Horn & Hardart Commissary. This was designed by Marshall and Fox (1917) and was an industrial building that was also later in its life the Chez Paree nightclub. With space for expansion there not being an option, Col. Pritzker's real estate division of Tawani Enterprises acquired the historic Monroe Building (1912) at the southwest corner of Michigan Avenue and Monroe Street. This Italian Gothic masonry high rise was the work of Holabird & Roche, as was their Gothic style University Club (1909) directly opposite on the northwest corner. Both equally massed buildings create a gateway to Millennium Park and the Art Institute of Chicago, a cultural heart of the city.

Holabird & Root restored the building and Atlanta-based TVS created the new libray and museum on the second and third floors, with museum offices on the fourth floor. Officially the Pritzker Military Library (now Pritzker Military Museum & Library/PMML) opened there in 2010. Public spaces done in Holabird & Root's restoration bring back the magnificence of the Rookwood tiled interiors whereas the TVS museum and library interiors are typified by extensive use of oak. A purpose-built iron and marble vintage-style staircase connects the institution's floors within the center of the stack areas. There is a club-like seating area as part of the main floor reading room, an oral history room, and open stack spaces, with a rare book room on the stack floor above. Exhibition areas are distributed throughout the interiors, with movable cases and display walls.

The PMML's great strength beyond its 53,000 volumes is a military poster collection that spans much of the twentieth century. Of special interest architecturally, are two additional spaces that relate to its strong video collection of Medal of Honor interviews. One is a permanent exhibition niche on the Medal of Honor which features the medal awarded to Hershel »Woody« Williams for his heroic actions during the Battle of Iwo Jima in 1945. The other is a state of the art, two-story auditorium and television broadcast facility. Book authors, military personalities, and Medal of Honor recipients are interviewed, those sessions being aired on public television and available through podcasts.

1. Monroe Building lobby. Photo: balloggphoto.com.
2–4. Museum interiors: entry, »Medal of Honor« exhibit, and auditorium. Photos: Pritzker Military Museum & Library.

MUSEUM & LIBRARY

REMEMBER
THE MAINE

**Bundeswehr Military History Museum/ Militärhistorisches Museum der Bundeswehr, Dresden, Germany. Renovation, 2011**
Daniel Libeskind; exhibition design: HG Merz and Barbara Holzer

Four American and British bombing raids February 13–15, 1945, and the resultant firestorm, destroyed 1,600 acres (647.49 ha) of Dresden's city center, killing approximately 25,000 people. The raids themselves have raised a firestorm of controversy since the war, with a wide divergence of opinions, ranging from their being a strategic necessity to a terror bombing display of power. The bombing destroyed a good portion of historic, mostly Baroque, architecture. Postwar reconstructions under the German Democratic Republic have continued through the current reunified Germany, the centerpiece being the Frauenkirche (1743), reconstructed and consecrated 2005. Further validation of historic reconstruction efforts in Dresden came through the 2018 Henry Hope Reed Award being given to Torsten Kulke, chair of the Gesellschaft Historischer Neumarkt Dresden . That organization has spearheaded the historic rebuilding of seventy sites in that district.

On the other hand, Dresden also has some striking contemporary buildings, best exemplified by the Ufa Cinema Center (1998) by Coop Himmelb(l)au and Daniel Libeskind's Militärhistorisches Museum der Bundeswehr or the Bundeswehr Military History Museum. In the latter, Libeskind created a bold repurposing of an 1876 arsenal which has been a military museum since 1897, and a museum of the German army since 1938. This is not to be confused with the Dresden Armory which is now the Deutsches Historisches Museum, having one of the world's largest collections of arms and armor. It is located within the castle whereas the military museum is situated to the north near the Dresden heath, which was not bombed. Rather than creating a museum that chronicles weapons and military events, Libeskind was commissioned a decade before the reopening to examine the nature of war in an almost anthropological way related to the origins and impact of conflict. The concrete, steel and glass wedge cut into the traditional Classicist building reinforces both the new interpretation through its bold design, and Libeskind's intention to characterize war as having catastrophic consequences.

The entire museum is said to be the largest in Germany, having 150,694 square feet (14,000 sq. m) of interior space holding more than 10,000 exhibits, and approximately 215,278 square feet (20,000 sq. m) of exterior display area for military vehicles. The five-storey wedge itself holds thematic spaces on War and Memory, War and Music, War and Theater, and War and Games. The exhibition design within is often as angular as Libeskind's frame. Galleries in spaces on either side of the wedge are more rectangular as one would expect within this traditional Classicist building. They hold a chronological sequence on the history of Germany's military. The wedge also holds a viewing platform 98 feet (30 m) high from which visitors can see the Frauenkirche at the city center about 2 miles (3 km) to the south. In addition to exhibition spaces and its collections of fine art, fire-arms and uniforms, the museum is known for its library and archive with thousands of relevant documents on the history of Germany's armed forces.

1. South façade at night. Photo: Volker Preusser/Alamy Stock Photo.
2. Museum model showing wedge integration. Photo: © Studio Libeskind.
3. Wedge interior. Photo: © Hufton+Crow Photography.

PEOPLE'S WAR

4. Chronological gallery.
5. Wedge theme gallery: »Military and Society – Toys«.
6. Wedge theme gallery: »Protection and Destruction«.
All photos: © Hufton+Crow Photography.

**Bletchley Park, Milton Keynes, England. Conservation of existing buildings and new visitor center, 2014**
Kennedy O'Callaghan Architects; conservation: Janie Price; exhibition design: Event Communications

Bletchley Park has gone down in history as well as popular culture as the place where secret Axis messages and codes were broken, allowing the Allied powers an intelligence advantage over their opponents in World War II. Popularized in media such as feature films *Enigma* (2001) and *Imitation Game* (2014), along with the television series *The Bletchley Circle* (2014 and later), we tend to think of the mansion house as the focal point of our image of the site. Indeed, Bletchley Park's house was expanded after 1883 into the Victorian pile we see today. The important point is not that home, but the buildings created on the grounds after Admiral Sir Hugh Sinclair acquired the home and 58 acres (23.47 ha) in 1938. As head of the Secret Intelligence Service then, he purchased the property himself for potential government use during what seemed to be an impending international conflict, essentially planning for the likelihood of the next world war. Situated near railroad lines that connected to think-tank universities, the site was to become a hub of Allied code breaking efforts during World War II. Approximately 10,000 people worked here, many with foreign language, cryptology, or electrical skills. These also included American cryptographers in the latter part of the war effort.

With British government efforts in full swing after the beginning of World War II in September 1939, more than twenty-five utilitarian buildings were constructed here. The wood frame ones were called huts and brick ones called blocks; huts had number suffixes and blocks had alphabetical ones. Different huts and blocks had different functions, many relating to cryptanalysis of the German Enigma cipher machine messages. There were, however, several huts devoted to a cafeteria and pub-like space, along with other recreational activities. The breaking of Enigma ciphers happened at Bletchley in Spring 1940 and continued success throughout the war in doing this was accomplished with help of the bombe. It and the machines Colossus and Tunny enabled personnel to examine the daily settings of various coded messages from a variety of German armed forces, giving access to thousands of enemy communications every day. At war's end, the buildings were used in a variety of ways, including for a teacher-training institute, eventually all of them falling into disrepair. After all, they were quickly constructed to win the war. With the Milton Keynes Borough Council support, the park was established as a conservation district and a trust was formed to maintain the buildings as a museum which was opened 1993.

Kennedy O'Callaghan Architects led the team in a conservation program of the huts, blocks and landscape, in close collaboration with Event Communications, creating a plan for the site's interpretation, all with funding from the Heritage Lottery Fund. This was developed 2010–14 and included repurposing a block into the visitor's center along with exhibitions within that and other structures on the site and mansion, totaling some 4,757 square feet (442 sq. m). The entire project cost £ 8 million from public and private sources of support. Work here continues to make improvements through 2025, further expanding public access to the site. The latest exhibition opened 2018 in Hut 11A on the invention of the bombe created by Alan Turing, Gordon Welchman and Harold Keen. Bletchley Park has an annual attendance of more than 250,000 visitors.

1. The Victorian Mansion. Photo: shutterstock.com.
2, 3. Block C – visitor center (top) and restored huts (bottom). Photos: ©Shaun Armstrong, mubsta.com.

pp. 78, 79
4, 5. Visitor-center interiors.
6. Restored hut exhibition interior.
All photos: © Shaun Armstrong, mubsta.com.

BLETCHLEYPARK

LSL
860

**Imperial War Museum, London, England.**
**Renovation, 2014**
Foster+Partners; exhibition design: Casson Mann

As discussed within this book's introduction, the Imperial War Museum/IWM represents, in many ways, the gold standard of military museums. The 1989 renovation set a new level by which to judge such institutions in its architecture as well as installations. And things only got better for the museum as it expanded to offsite locations beyond its Lambeth Road location in London. As good as its 1980s renovation was, it was looking dated over more than fifteen years later, despite innovative temporary installations and new exhibition wings such as that for the Holocaust Gallery (1996) designed by Stephen Greenberg of DEGW. Foster was selected as the architect with the initial phase of the three-year renovation scheduled to coincide with the Centennial of World War I in 2014. His firm and exhibition designers Casson Mann, the latter also working on the exhibits for the IWM's Churchill War Rooms, reconfigured the main entry atrium and the World War I galleries in a £ 40 million project.

The World War I galleries are on the ground floor and visitors can eventually ascend through the building's levels in chronological exhibitions that will end at the topmost level with contemporary subjects. Foster's firm also moved the café and museum store to the lowest level off the atrium, with the café having access to the park and open to outside traffic when the museum is closed. Previously blocked windows were now opened with views to the park. Within the atrium, aircraft and other large artifacts are still suspended or projected from the vaulted structure above, though an angular ceiling covers them atop. Unlike the previous hanging arrangement of the 1980s, objects now are presented at their appropriate chronological levels related to exhibit floors above. When viewed from those levels, large concrete piers or »fins« frame the displayed aircraft and provide angular entries to the gallery levels from a steel staircase within the atrium.

Over 400 objects are displayed within this core organizing space, more than 60 never having been shown before. Their interpretation focuses on each one's individual history often related to specific people and events. This is contrasted with the previous 1980s installation which displayed a potpourri of militaria for fans and enthusiasts. The consistent new interpretation overall relates to what the museum calls the causes, course and consequence of wars, paralleling the interpretive paths of other museums such as the Militärhistorisches Museum der Bundeswehr (2011) in Dresden (see. p. 72). It is evident in the IWM's new World War I gallery which covers not only 1914 to 1918, but the wider context of 1900–29. As for the atrium redesign, the director general Diane Lees likens it to an upgrade appropriate to a new public building and not a utilitarian structure as before. She has been quoted as having one of the museum's long-term plans relate to more fine art exhibitions, particularly contemporary art in relation to like conflicts, in order to continue to expand their audience. This is something that the museum has done consistently well back through several decades.

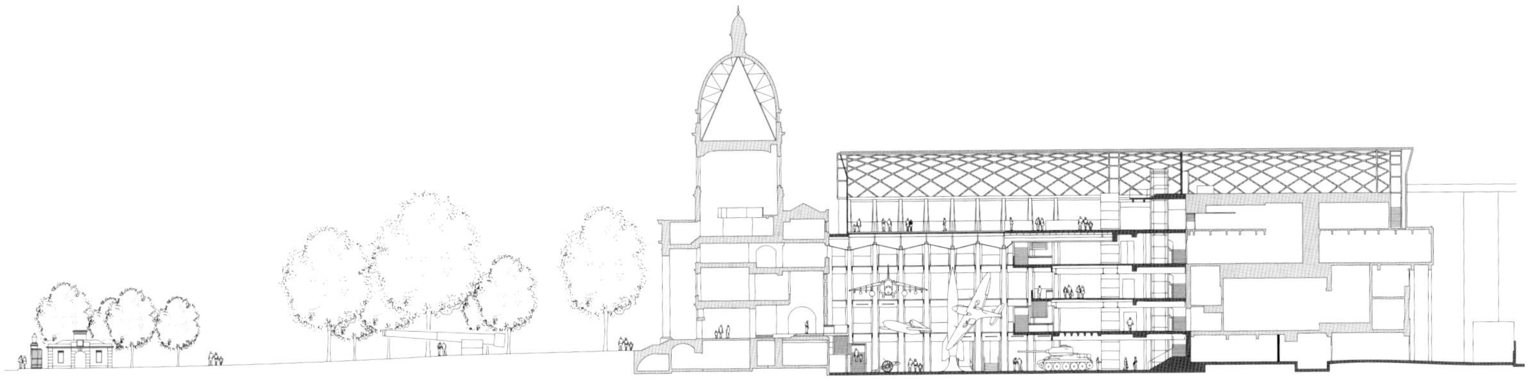

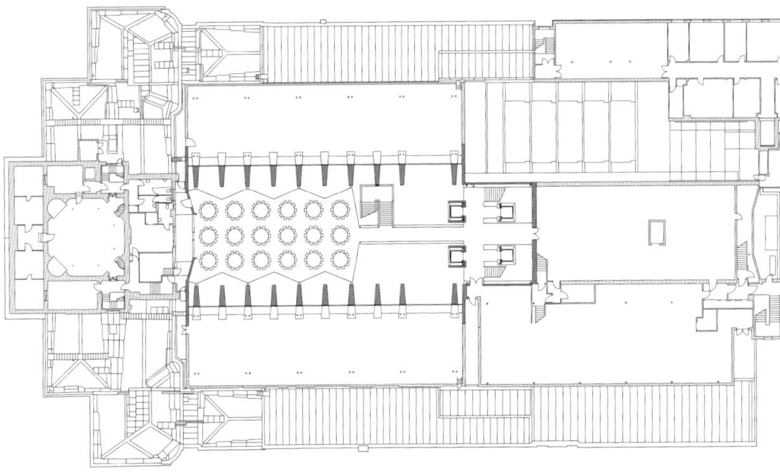

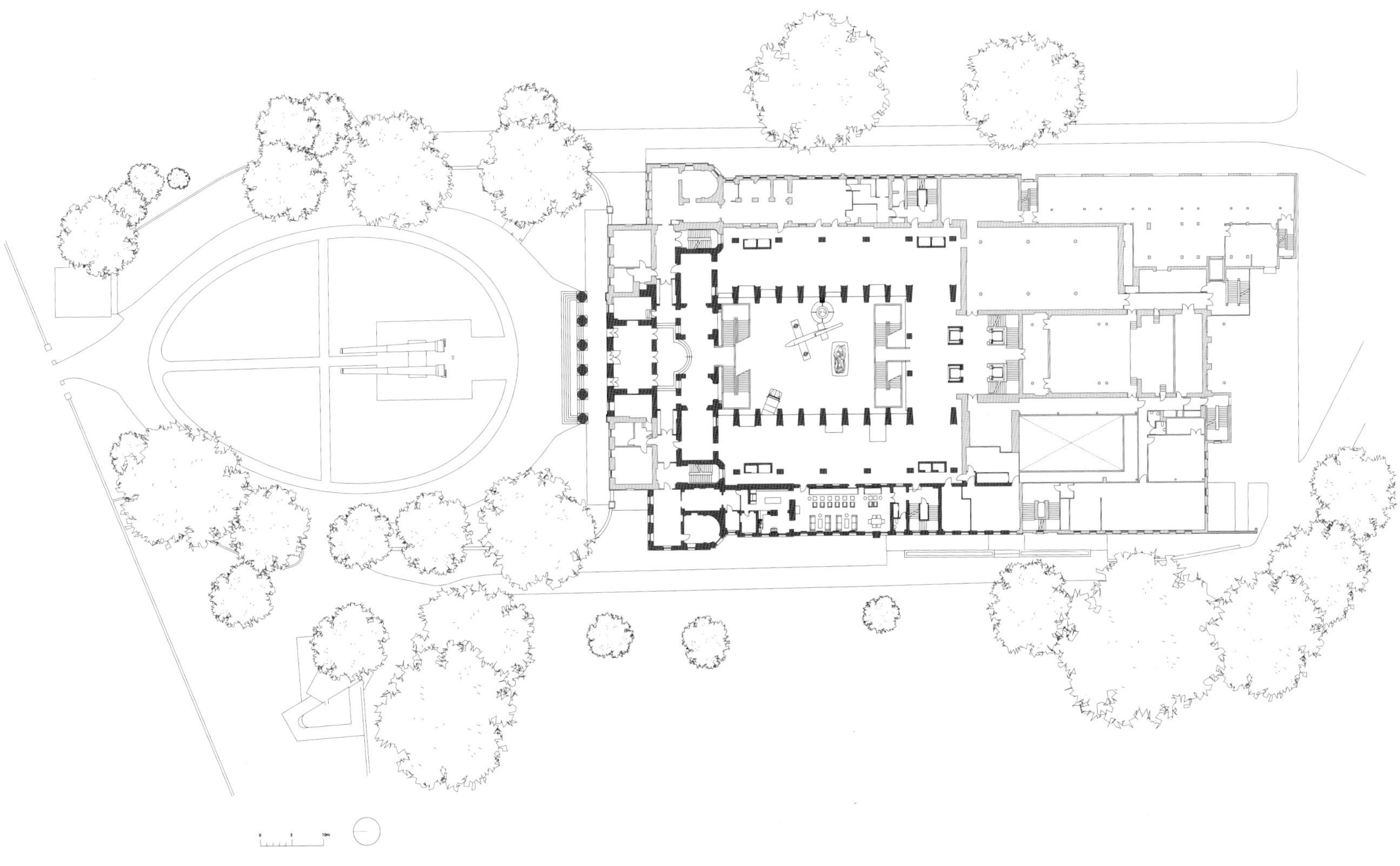

pp. 80, 81
1. View into renovated atrium lobby, showing Harrier jet in the foreground and Spitfire in the background. Photo: © Nigel Young, Foster + Partners.
2. Longitudinal section and plans. Photo: © Foster + Partners.

3, 4. Renovated atrium lobby space views, with suspended aircraft such as a Harrier jet, Spitfire, and V1 cruise missile as well as a cutaway display of a V2 missile, among other artifacts. Photos: © Nigel Young, Foster+Partners.

pp. 84, 85
5,6. Views into the atrium lobby through a small weapons display as well as up to the suspended angular ceiling. Photos: © Nigel Young, Foster+Partners.

**Nationaal Militair Museum/National Military Museum, Soesterberg, The Netherlands, 2014**
Felix Claus Dick van Wageningen Architects; exhibition design. Kossmann.dejong

The National Military Museum/NMM is the museum dedicated to the Dutch armed forces, combining the collections of principally their army and air force. The new museum was a multi-year project headed by the Heijmans PPP consortium to create an integrated visitor experience of landscape and museum on the former Soesterberg air base. This facility dates to 1911 back to the dawn of aviation in the Netherlands, and was an active base until closing in 2008. It is approximately eighteen miles (29 km) northeast of Utrecht. The architects worked with the exhibition designers from Kossmann.dejong and landscape architects from H+N+S to create this coordinated project covering more than 111 acres (45 ha).

The building itself planned 2011–13 and constructed 2013/j10ß414 contains some 215,278 square feet (20,000 sq. m). Its steel frame, open space, and glazed walls are akin to large American convention center spaces such as that of Ludwig Mies van der Rohe's design in the 1950s and its somewhat comparable realization in McCormick Place, Chicago (1971) by Gene Summers with Helmut Jahn of C.F. Murphy Associates. The architects at Soesterberg stressed visual dialogue in their design, dialogue within as well as outside to the landscape. Their building has a large span steel framework more than 820 x 360 feet (250 x 110 m). The big windows measure about 42 feet high by 16 feet wide (13 x 5 m). An observation tower projects above the building roof at more than 100 feet (30 m) high above ground level. The steel structure and large open space permit hanging large artifacts from above, thereby increasing exhibition volume. The roof carries 3,240 photovoltaic panels to increase the building's energy efficiency. The landscape architects combined several approaches within the overall site, from a nature area, fog fen, and heath to memorial garden and ecological forest. Their landscape plan integrates existing air base structures, historic bomb craters, and using gabions for retaining walls.

Inside the museum, visitors have two different experiences created by the architects and especially the exhibition designers. One relates to daylight viewing of military hardware – vehicles and aircraft – in the »Arsenal« near the large-scale windows. The exhibition designers arranged five jet age aircraft in a looping »dogfight« sequence, adding an imaginative dynamic variety to the display. The other is a black box on the upper level which showcases the history of the military within Dutch society from the Middle Ages through today. These are thematic spaces where artifacts are animated by media presentations and effects, making the stories about individual objects and people come alive for the visitor. The designers also created an »Xplore« interactive exhibition space for families with children on the lower level underneath the thematic historical sections on the upper level. In addition to those exhibition spaces that showcase more than 3,000 artifacts, the museum has a café on the ground floor and an auditorium at the upper level that overlooks the »Arsenal«.

Heijmans manages the museum for the Ministry of Defence under a twenty-five year contract. The museum was planned to accommodate 200,000 visitors annually and in the first three months of operation, they exceeded this count. The total cost of the project was 130 million Euros.

1, 2. General view and detail showing suspended C-47 transport. Photo: © Christian Richters Photography.
3. Exhibition plan, main level. Photo: Kossmann.dejong.

T 443
UN
UN

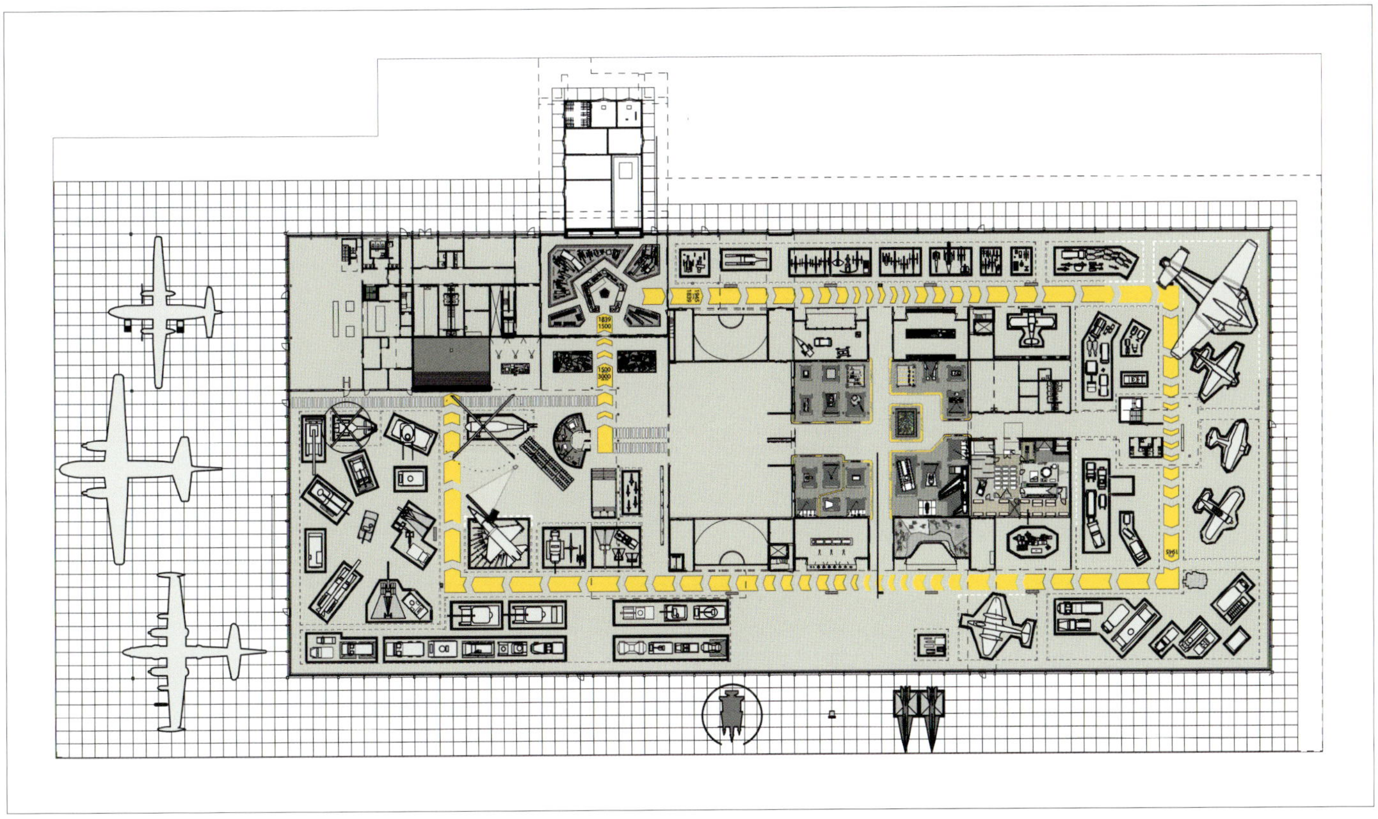

4. Main hall »Arsenal«. Photo: © Christian Richters Photography.
5. Main floor exhibition installation »dogfight«, showing NF-5A fighter plane above AMX-13 tank. Photo: © Thijs Wolzak, courtesy Kossmann.dejong.

K-3020
NL

DE WAPENHANDELAARS VAN DE WERELD
GLOBAL ARMS TRADERS

6. Netherlands theme space. Photo: © Thijs Wolzak, courtesy Kossmann.dejong.
7. Treasury. Photo: © Thijs Wolzak, courtesy Kossmann.dejong.
8. »Xplore« interactive zone, main floor. Photo: © Christian Richters Photography.

**National Museum of the United States Air Force, Dayton, Ohio, USA. Building 4, 2016**
BRPH Architects and Turner Construction Co. Design Build

Wright Patterson Air Force Base northeast of Dayton, Ohio, was established officially in 1948. It began life as the Wilbur Wright Field and Dayton's McCook Field in 1917. Both merged in 1927 with the closure of McCook. The base has served as a research and testing facility for aircraft back through its World War I inception, if not before. The Wright Brothers in fact tested their own early aircraft 1904/05 on Huffman Prairie, which became part of base land during World War I.

Early army aircraft as well as other artifacts became the basis of the museum collection at McCook Field in 1923. In 1935, the museum opened its first building with funding from the Works Progress Administration during the Great Depression. The building was used for military purposes during World War II with the collection removed to storage. After World War II, the collection, including captured Axis aircraft tested at the field, was reinstalled in Building 89, a hangar on the base that was officially accessible by the public in 1955. Attendance then was 41, 662.

With this building not appropriate to museum climate control, the Air Force Museum Foundation, established 1960, raised funds to construct a new facility at the edge of the base. Eero Saarinen was originally commissioned. In 1964, he proposed a trapezoidal building with a large wing-like canopy roof to cost approximately $ 10 to 12 million. This was deemed too costly to construct, so in 1970 the foundation contracted the Pascoe Steel Corporation of Columbus, Georgia, and Cleveland architects Dalton, Dalton and Little to redesign it. What was constructed was a large-span, hangar-like building of more than 192,000 square feet (17,837.38 sq. m). This $ 6.5 million structure on a 400 acres (161.88 ha) site opened in 1971 and was designed to accommodate 100 aircraft. *The New York Times* (September 5, 1971) reported on its construction and opening, its first year of operation said have included over 600,000 visitors.

Since then through today, the complex has witnessed a series of expansions, mostly through repetitive hangar-like buildings that connect to the original 1971 structure. In addition, they incorporated a 500 seat IMAX theater off the original building in 1991. The expandable plan permitted the construction of yet another large span hangar 2014–16 at the cost of $ 40.8 million. As with all other constructions before, the private-non-profit foundation raised the construction costs and museum operations are run by the Air Force. This new Building 4 was designed by BRPH, an American firm familiar with large industrial and commercial projects but also with theme park design and construction. Some of its major work is also aviation related such as the Delta IV Launch Complex at Cape Canaveral and Boeing's 787 Final Assembly Building in North Charleston, South Carolina. Their Building 4 at the museum has 224,000 square feet (20,810.28 sq. m) mostly dedicated to the larger aircraft, including presidential planes, a space shuttle trainer (CCT-1), and a Science Technology Engineering and Math/STEM learning center. The building itself achieved Leadership in Energy and Environmental Design /LEED Gold status for its energy efficiency. Although contracted exhibition designers and fabricators occasionally work here, the museum has an in-house staff for most exhibition designs. 829,424 visitors came to the museum in 2017 to see their more than 360 aircraft on exhibit.

1. First building for the Air Force museum, Area B, Building 12, Wright Patterson Air Force Base. Photo: Historic American Engineering Record, Library of Congress.
2. Aerial view of initial building module, 1971. Photo: United States Air Force.
3. Aerial view of museum buildings, left to right, from 1971 through 2016. Photo: Ken La Rock, United States Air Force.

4,5. Aerial views, including one with a Curtiss JN4 Jenny fly over, showing the museum entry and 1991 IMAX theater to the left of the main halls. Photos: Jim Copes and Victoria Thomas (fly over), both United States Air Force.
6. Interior of Building 4, 2016, showing at the center Air Force One (26000) used by Presidents Kennedy, Johnson and Nixon. Photo: Ken La Rock, United States Air Force.

UNITED STATES OF AMERICA
26000

**Museum of the American Revolution, Philadelphia, Pennsylvania, USA, 2017**
Robert A. M. Stern Architects; exhibition design: MFM Design, HealyKohler Design, Maltbie

Robert A. M. Stern is best known for his traditional designs over the past four decades, even when it is not fashionable to design that way for a number of today's architects who are attuned to computer-generated organic forms. Stern's firm has done a number of historically contextual university buildings and libraries, along with museums such as the Norman Rockwell Museum (1993) in Stockbridge, Massachusetts, the International Storytelling Center (2002) in Jonesborough, Tennessee, the Perkins Visitor Center at Wave Hill (2004) in the Bronx, New York, and the George W. Bush Presidential Center (2013) in Dallas. Stern, with his firm's design partners Alexander P. Lamis, who also worked on the Bush Presidential Center, and Kevin M. Smith, began work on the Museum of the American Revolution in 2011. Groundbreaking took place three years after. Planning for the museum began in 2000. The trustees implemented a successful $ 173 million campaign to build and provide $ 48 million in endowment to help manage this facility.

In this project, Stern created a compatible and appropriately scaled building within the context of Philadelphia's important brick structures of the eighteenth century, many being tangible architectural sites related to the American War of Independence. The new building is an homage to the past but also intended as a reinterpretation for the present. The grand staircase off the museum's lobby epitomizes this. Its form is meant to be residential in origin and scale but also monumental in being capable of securely holding more than a hundred museum visitors. The three-story building totals 118,000 square feet (10,962.56 sq. m). The main floor has a museum store and café that open to the street, as well as a ticketing lobby, a 175-person capacity theater, and a temporary exhibit space of 5,000 square feet (464.50 sq. m). The top floor contains »Liberty Hall«, a double-height programmatic and entertaining space for museum events. The second floor houses the permanent collection within a 16,000 square feet (1,486 sq. m) exhibit designed to immerse visitors into the history of the American Revolution. Perhaps one of the most interesting facts related to the museum's construction was the discovery of some 82,000 artifacts from the seventeenth and eighteenth centuries that were found when the site was excavated for the building's foundations. The bulk of these were transferred to the State Museum of Pennsylvania, though some are on display in the museum.

HealyKohler Design in Washington, D.C., created the graphics and the overall exhibition design. The New Jersey firm of Maltbie was the exhibit fabricator and installed the exhibits. George Washington's Headquarters War Tent is displayed within a dedicated theater experience developed by Donna Lawrence Productions. The rare artifact is protected in a climate-controlled environment that is revealed after a short film about it. Exhibits with realistic life-cast mannequins and recreated environments such as the famed »Liberty Tree« and privateer ship deck, the latter built by Philadelphia's own Independence Seaport Museum, are interpreted with actual artifacts as well as interactives and large-scale graphics. The museum officially opened April 19, 2017 on the anniversary of the first battles of the war in 1775 at Lexington and Concord in Massachusetts. Since its opening, more than 370,000 people have visited the museum.

1. Chestnut Street façade. Relief sculptures of famed history paintings, *Washington Crossing the Delaware* (left) and *The Signing of the Declaration of Independence* (right), flank a bay window that gives passersby a view into the museum's lobby.
2, 3. Grand staircase and upper museum level.
Photos: Peter Aaron, OTTO.

ARMS OF INDEPENDENCE
1775–1783
The Field of Battle
SEPTEMBER 11, 177
00:00

4. Exhibit casework. Photo: Peter Aaron, OTTO.
5. »Liberty Tree Exhibition« in »Resistance« themed gallery. Photo: Dan Husted, Maltbie.

**First Division Museum, Wheaton, Illinois, USA. Renovation, 2017**
DLA Architects, Inc.; exhibition design: Luci Creative

Most architectural enthusiasts know about the 1922 international competition to build the Chicago Tribune tower, organized by that newspaper's publisher, Robert R. McCormick. But not that many know that he was a decorated American army artillery officer in World War I. During the war, McCormick served as a Lt. Colonel (promoted to full Colonel afterwards) with the First Infantry Division. He fought in the Battle of Cantigny May 28, 1918 and was evacuated to Paris and the United States, after being gassed there as well as recuperating from the Spanish flu pandemic. He renamed his own estate in 1919 after Cantigny in France, at the first reunion of division veterans there. This was the first successful American offensive in that war, offering proof, to French and British allies, of the United States Army's worth in battle.

McCormick's Cantigny is today a 500 acres (202.35 ha) park funded by the McCormick Charitable Trust. It contains his classical revival museum-home, an adjacent golf course, picnic groves, restaurant, as well as formal and less formal gardens. It was opened to the public in 1958, three years after McCormick's death. Moreover, it is the home of the First Infantry Division Museum, originally built 1960 within the estate's renovated stables by architect Andrew Rebori. He was a lifelong friend of McCormick who also designed the granite memorial exedra on the grounds for McCormick and his wife, dedicated 1957. The *Chicago Tribune* (April 1, 1959) reported that this initial museum had immersive full-scale dioramas created by the industrial design firm of Latham Tyler Jensen Inc., whose partners were proteges of Raymond Loewy. The tradition of large scale dioramas continues in subsequent museum displays here through today.

The First Division Museum was built anew in 1992/93 by architects VOA Associates (now Stantec) into a 38,000 square feet (3,530.30 sq. m) museum and research center. The museum is perhaps best known for its collection of American tanks from World War I through today, with examples such as an M1917, based on a Renault FT-17, up through the M1 Abrams of our era. These are displayed on the museum grounds in a Tank Park of fifteen armored vehicles and artillery pieces. Beyond that the museum has a number of historical army vehicles that include a Willys MB Jeep and M3 Halftrack, both from World War II. These are operable and are brought out for various displays in the summer months.

To commemorate the division's creation during World War I, the museum underwent an $ 8.5 million exhibition renovation that opened August 2017. The 2,500 square feet (232 sq. m) space formerly used for temporary exhibitions and programs was reopened with an exhibition titled »Duty First«. This focuses on the various types of missions in which the division engages, up through today. Interactives created by Luci Creative are featured here, their intent being to demonstrate a soldier's experience. The exhibit has over fifteen integrated media and interactives that incorporate on-camera interviews. The existing permanent exhibition which is a series of chronological dioramas on the division's history was also renovated by those designers. They kept those basic installations from the past and improved on them through immersive experiences. This newly redone »First in War« exhibit incorporates and updates full scale vignettes such as the World War I trench, Omaha Beach landing, Battle of the Bulge, and Vietnam jungle combat. Ravenswood Studio was the exhibition fabricator on the job. Before its new renovation, the museum would have over 175,000 visitors a year despite being some thirty-five miles (56.33 km) west of Chicago. With the exhibition updates, it is expected that this annual number will increase.

1. Stuart (foreground) and Bulldog (background) tanks on the museum's grounds. Photo: courtesy First Division Museum.
2. Museum exterior. Photo: courtesy First Division Museum.
3. Museum lobby and entry to »First in War« exhibit. Photo: © Matt Kosterman, courtesy Luci Creative.

pp. 102, 103
4. »Duty First« exhibit.
5. »First in War« exhibit: Vietnam.
6. »First in War« exhibit: D-Day in World War II.
Photos: © Matt Kosterman, courtesy Luci Creative.

FIRST IN WAR

PEACEKEEPING
1996
EXPLORE THE STORIES OF 1 ID SOLDIERS
DWIGHT CHURCH

GETTING READY TO LEAVE

spill out into waist-deep water,

**National Army Museum, London, England. Renovation, 2017**
BDP Architects; exhibition design: Event Communications and PLB

London's National Army Museum was the brainchild of Field Marshall Sir Gerald Templer, decorated veteran of both World Wars, who spearheaded creation of this institution which was chartered in 1960. The current building originally designed by William Holford & Partners was begun in 1961 and completed 1971. Paralleling the Imperial War Museum's expansion plans with the IWM North in Manchester (see p. 26), the National Army Museum also intended, in 2002, to build a branch budgeted at £ 19 million approximately 240 miles (386 km) north of London near Catterick. Initial plans were created by architects Austin-Smith:Lord but this project was postponed and then cancelled. Instead, the museum administration focused on redefining its mission as regards reconnecting the army with society, explaining the role of the army to visitors, and using the collections to communicate the army's and soldiers' stories, past and present. This also included renovation of its London building and a complete refreshing of the exhibitions within. In 2014 the museum was awarded an £ 11 million Heritage Lottery Fund/HLF grant. The museum also fundraised to a total of £ 23.75 million from the Ministry of Defence, the Foyle Foundation and City Bridge Trust, and others for the redevelopment of this building.

BDP Architects with Event Communications were appointed in 2011 to redesign the museum over 2014–17. BDP dates back to Professor Sir George Grenfell Baines. He began his own firm in 1937, as well as the Building Design Partnership/BDP in 1961, founded by Baines and John Wilkinson, Arnold Towler and Bill White, in five studio locations across England. Today they have offices across the world. Recent cultural sector works include the National Maritime Museum's Neptune Court (1999), Kelvingrove Art Gallery in Glasgow (2005), Shetland Museum and Archives (2007), and gallery redesign at the British Museum (2008). BDP's work at the National Army Museum focused on making the visitor experience more transparent in moving the entry more directly to Royal Hospital Road, glazing the entire ground floor level, and including a street-accessible café at the northwest corner.

Moreover, they, with Event Communications, reconfigured the interior to create an atrium as the organizing space to galleries and public services. The new installation includes some 2,500 artifacts, graphic displays, and interactives arranged thematically in galleries related to Soldier, Army, Battle, Society and Insight. The Soldier Gallery is on the main floor with the Insight Gallery and Kid's Play base on the lower ground floor. Galleries for the Army, Battle and Society are all on the upper floor. The topmost floor above is for museum access only – staff and board of trustees. The finished museum opened to the public on March 31, 2017, with never seen before artifacts such as the Duke of Wellington's cloak, Lawrence of Arabia's robes, and the skeleton of Napoleon's horse. More importantly, the thematic sections, particularly the ones on Society and Soldier, fulfilled their mission intentions to connect the role of the army to visitors today. Before closing for reconstruction, the museum witnessed 247,000 annually and with its renovation, museum officials hope for an annual visitorship of some 400,000.

1. Exterior, detail. Photo: © Nick Caville, BDP.
2. Section and ground-floor plan. Photo: © BDP.

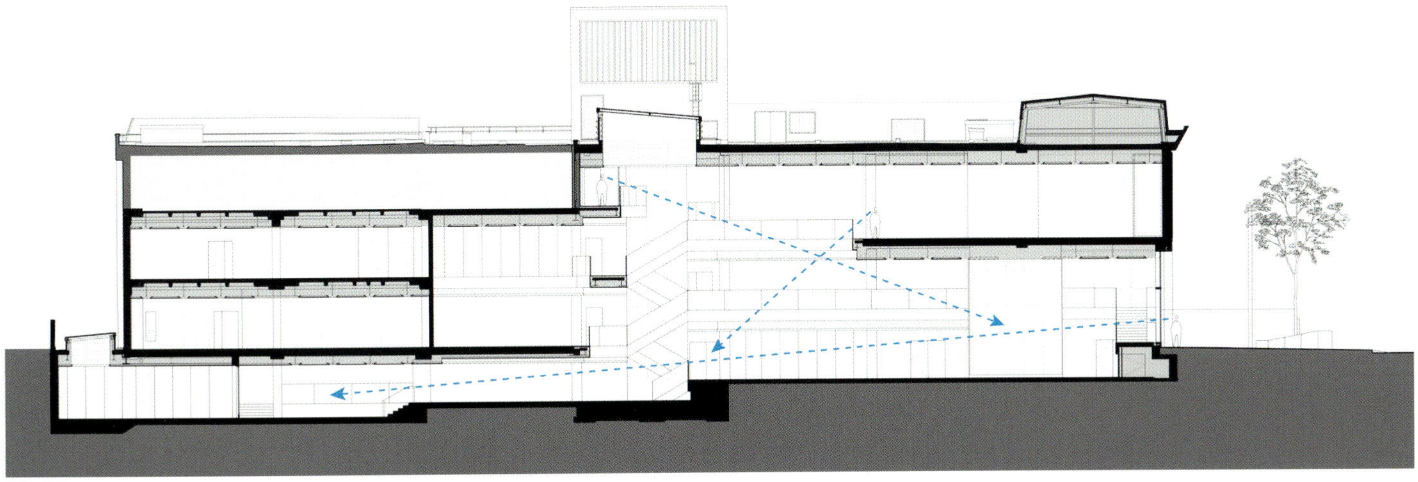

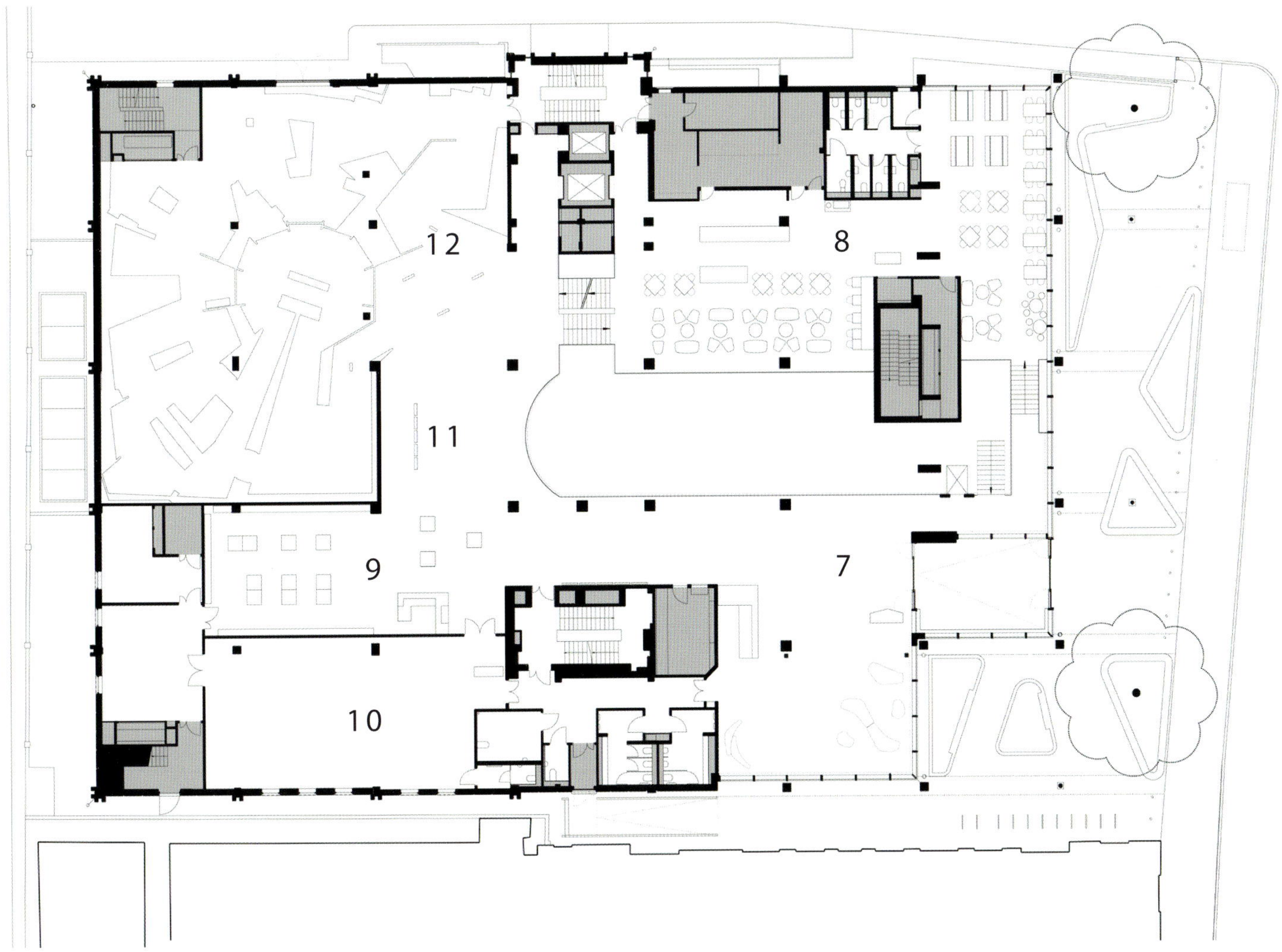


7. RECEPTION & FOYER
8. CAFE
9. SHOP
10. PLAY BASE
11. INTRODUCTION GALLERY
12. SOLDIER GALLERY

3,4. Museum atrium and upper-floor exhibition entry to »Society and the Army«. Photo: © Nick Caville, BDP.
5. Weapons display in the »Battle« Gallery. Photo: ukartpics/Alamy Stock Photo.

**Museum of the Second World War, Gdańsk, Poland, 2017**
Studio Architektoniczne Kwadrat; exhibition design: Tempora

Danzig, now Gdańsk, was created a Free City after World War I's Treaty of Versailles, the city being under the protection of the League of Nations. Technically removed from Germany it was also neither part of Poland, though Poland had customs use of the port. With the rise of the Nazi party in Germany during 1933 the same essentially happened in Danzig with its majority German population. Politically the city became more attuned to Germany than Poland, especially as signs of war approached in 1939, and especially with the German invasion of Poland on September 1 of that year. The city was officially annexed by Germany in October 1939 and liberated by the Red Army on March 30, 1945. Much of Gdańsk lay in ruins at war's end, its geographic jurisdiction being transferred back to Poland at the Yalta Conference of February 1945. It may seem a bit odd that a World War II Museum would be built here more than seven decades after the conflict's end, but many cite the Battle of Weserplatte and defence of the post office in Gdańsk as the first battles of the war on the very day of the invasion as reason enough for this construction.

With that context in mind, an international competition was held in 2010 to design a war memorial museum on approximately 2.5 acres (1 ha) of a site on the Nowa Radunia canal, north of the old town's historic St. Mary's Church. Of the more than 127 entries, the jury selected one by Studio Kwadrat, citing its contemporary monumentality and attraction-like design akin to that of historic structures like St. Mary's. Kwadrat was founded by Jacek Droszcz and others in 1989. He and Bazyli Domsta lead the firm today. It was Jacek's idea to create the angularly tilted 133 feet (40.5 m) tower to mark the site, with most of the 247, 570 square feet (23,000 sq. m) museum below. This creates a public plaza with exhibits underneath. The angular spaces in the museum and the tower above were meant to be suggestive of war's disruption but perhaps not as overtly so as in some other contemporary museums. The tower itself was planned for commercial use regarding a café and restaurant atop. The museum was constructed 2012–17 with a budget of 100 million Euros. The overall red texture from the outside includes rubble from some of Gdańsk's buildings as well as large dyed concrete slabs.

Visitors descend into a multi-story grey concrete atrium to enter the museum lobby, which has the ticket counters, café, bookstore, 115 seat theater, and a wood paneled 300 seat auditorium. Adjacent is an exhibit hall of 16,404 square feet (1,524 sq. m). The architect's idea in placing a war museum underground relates to the essential evils of conflict versus the rays of hope as you ascend back unto the light. Gdynia designers Loft planned and furnished most of the public interiors and the Brussels firm of Tempora created the diorama-like immersive exhibition spaces that house some 2,000 artifacts. These include excavations from the site such as paving stones from the city's Grosse Gasse. The museum opened March 23, 2017 and within two weeks it had some 14,000 visitors. A court case against the museum administration by the new government soon after that opening led to the merger of this institution with one not yet created that would focus more on the Polish perspective of the war, rather than the more international one within the exhibits at opening. Regardless, the museum has certainly made its mark, architecturally, in the world of new military museums and has an active educational and exhibit program today.

1, 2. Panorama of the museum and view of the tower at the Nowa Radunia canal off the Motlawa River. Photos: Tom Kurek, courtesy Studio Architektoniczne Kwadrat.

pp. 110, 111
3,4. Site plan and section. Photos: courtesy Studio Architektoniczne Kwadrat.
5. Bridge connecting the museum tower (left) with offices. Photo: Tom Kurek, courtesy Studio Architektoniczne Kwadrat.

pp. 112, 113
6–8. Museum lobby, auditorium and staircase. Photos: Tom Kurek, courtesy Studio Architektoniczne Kwadrat.

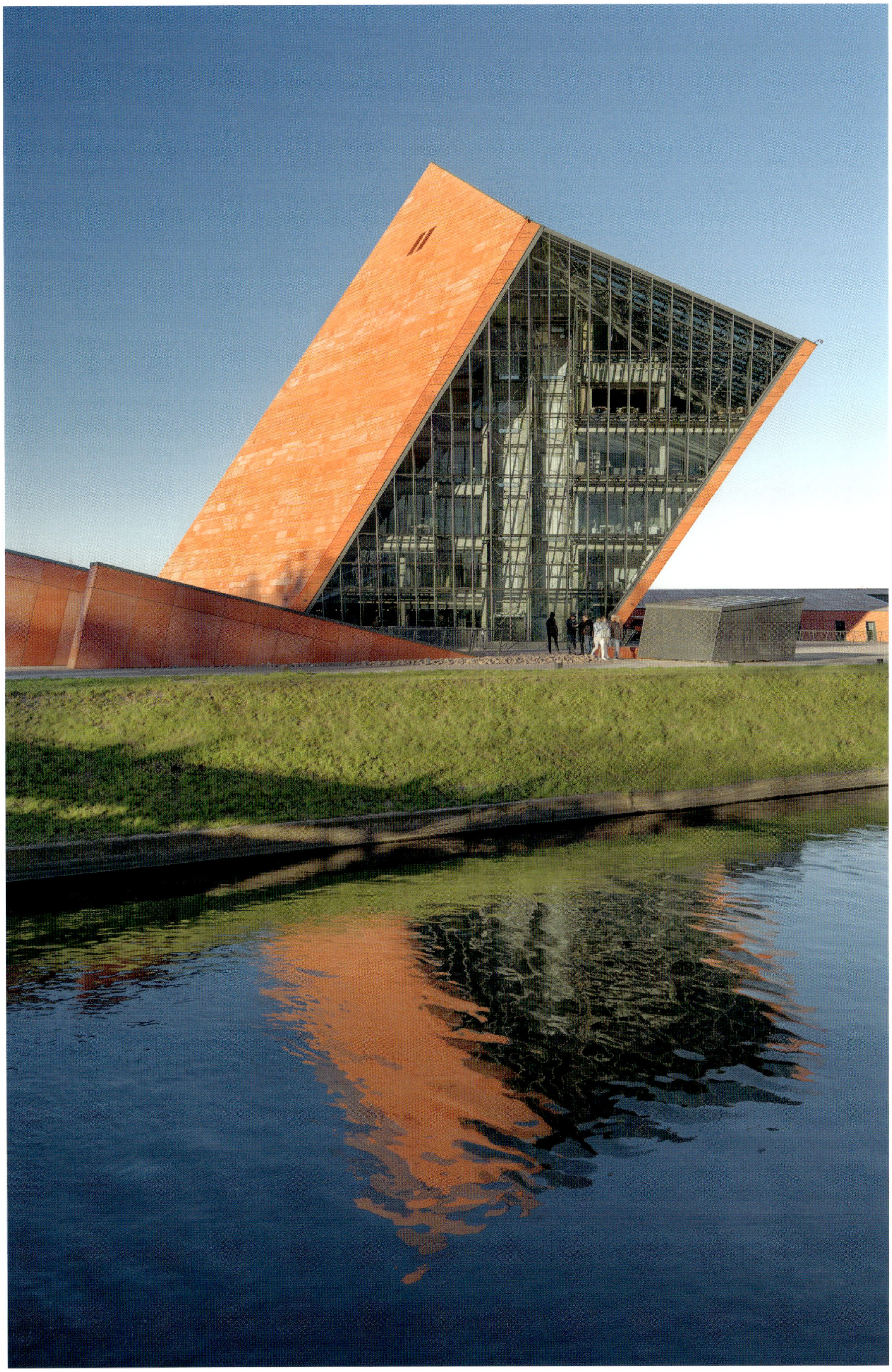

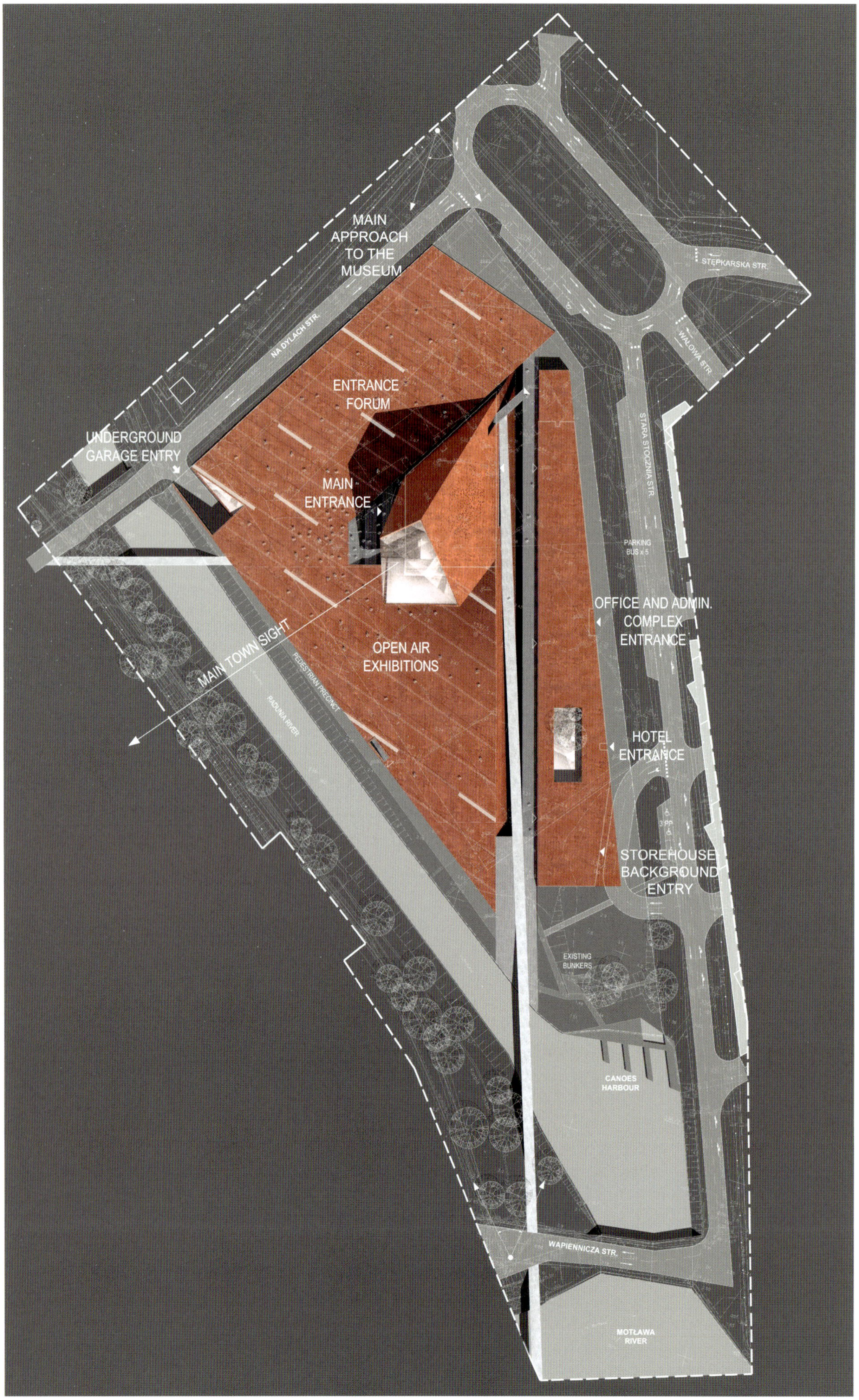
MAIN APPROACH TO THE MUSEUM
NA DYLACH STR.
STĘPKARSKA STR.
WAŁOWA STR.
STARA STOCZNIA STR.
ENTRANCE FORUM
UNDERGROUND GARAGE ENTRY
MAIN ENTRANCE
PARKING BUS x 5
OFFICE AND ADMIN. COMPLEX ENTRANCE
OPEN AIR EXHIBITIONS
MAIN TOWN SIGHT
PEDESTRIAN PRECINCT
RADUNA RIVER
HOTEL ENTRANCE
STOREHOUSE BACKGROUND ENTRY
EXISTING BUNKERS
CANOES HARBOUR
WAPIENNICZA STR.
MOTŁAWA RIVER

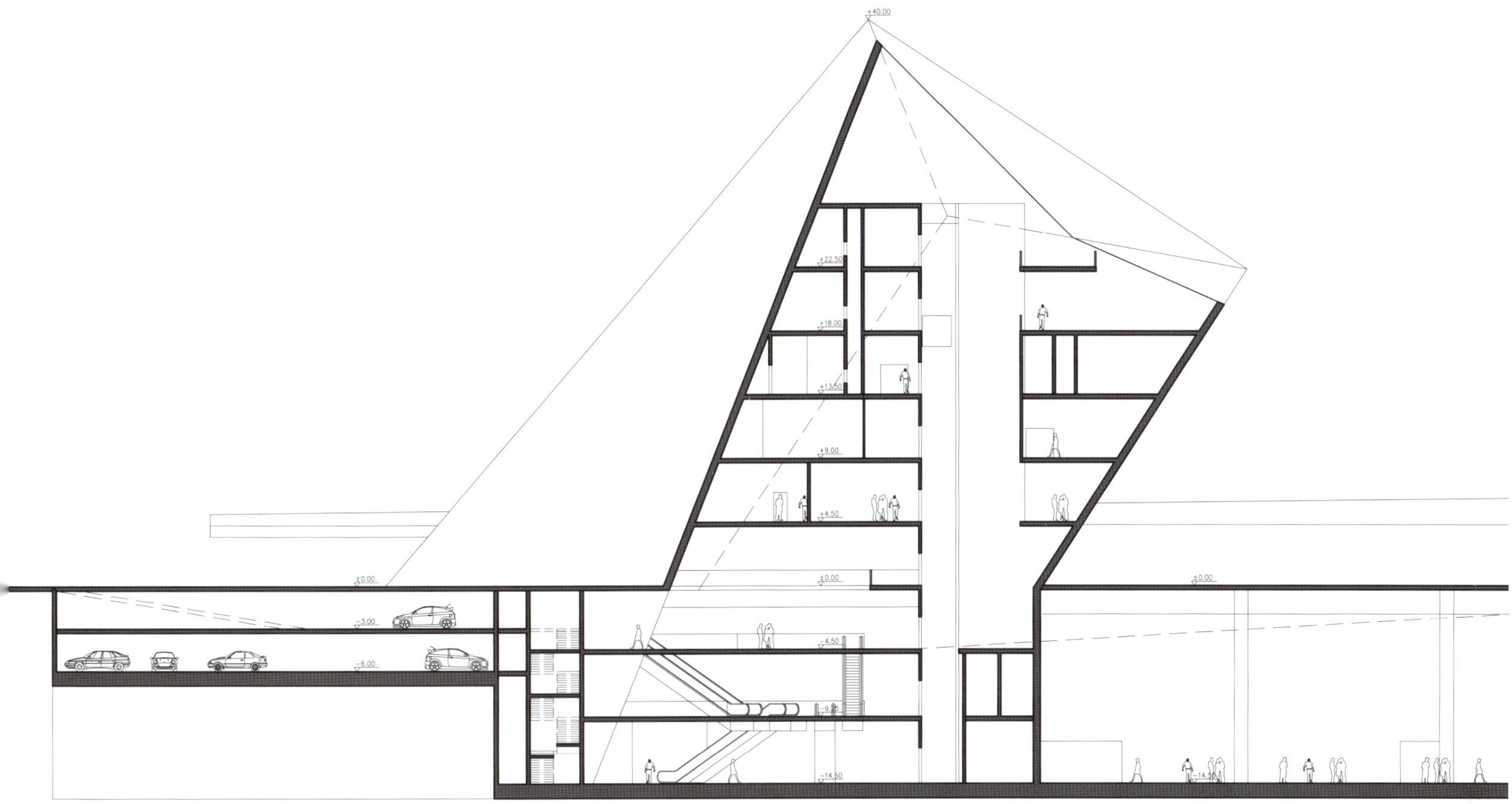
+40.00
+22.50
+18.00
+13.50
+9.00
+4.50
±0.00
-3.00
-6.00
-4.50
-9.25
-14.50

**National World War II Museum, New Orleans, Louisiana, USA, 2018**
Voorsanger Mathes LLC; exhibition design: Gallagher & Associates

Over a span of more than one and half decades the museum has led a sizable team of consultants to completely redefine the National D-Day Museum in New Orleans as it expanded to The National WWII Museum. The mission was to not only rebrand the museum, but to fully redevelop the audience, the storeyline, and the use of collections and technology. The client aimed to tell the story of the American experience in the war that changed the world – why it was fought, how it was won, and what it means today – so that all generations would understand the price of freedom and be inspired by what they learn. Gallagher & Associates alongside project architect Voorsanger Mathes LLC, developed a deep understanding of the sacrifices made by those who fought for our freedom, enabling the designers to interpret the stories of World War II in a way that personalizes and celebrates these individuals.

Design architect Bart Voorsanger said: »The war's frightening losses, duration, the liberation of millions, demanded an architecture of emotional reciprocity. We proposed individual pavilions of phased construction surrounding a parade ground. Their architecture emerged as a materiality of large interlocking concrete, glass and ribbed metal metaphorically offering protection for our troops but with a visual density bridging on intimidation. Soaring twelve stories over the parade ground is the Canopy of Peace (2018), uniting the campus emblematically for all nationalities, celebrating and honoring those who fought for our freedom.«

The resultant master plan involved the construction of six new buildings within a museum campus, including a 4D theater, signature restaurant and live entertainment venue, retail, and a hotel. The campus includes the first building, the Louisiana Memorial Pavilion, showcasing large artifacts of the war and exhibits on D-Day, the Home Front, and the Radio-Frequency Identification/RFID Dog Tag Experience; the Solomon Victory Theater Complex, featuring a 4D theater experience designed by the Hettema Group showcasing the exclusive Tom Hanks production, »Beyond All Boundaries«, and »BB's Stage Door Canteen«; Campaigns of Courage, which explores both the European-Mediterranean and Asia-Pacific campaigns of the war; the US Freedom Pavilion: The Boeing Center; the John E. Kushner Restoration Pavilion where staff and volunteers restore artifacts in public view; and more.

In designing the exhibitions for the Campaigns of Courage Pavilion, Patrick Gallagher, Rob Malootian, and Carl Rhodes with other team members of Gallagher Associates aspired to create a gritty and personal account of the war's progress. Archival video footage is projected onto a variety of meticulously-recreated theatrical environments which evoke various battlefront locales, including the snow-covered Ardennes forest, an abandoned German bunker, the jungles of Guadalcanal, the Marianas cliffs of Saipan, and destroyed buildings of Manilla. In contrast to the more tactile physical environments, the design team employed a minimal and consistent system for printed graphics and based the design of artifact cases on U.S. supply crates. Integral to the experience is an RFID Dog Tag component, which allows visitors to select a service member from either the European or Pacific campaigns and follow their story through interactive stations and call-out moments. Each location features a prominent quote, a paragraph of text, and a collection of photographs, video clips, and/or oral histories related to the servicemember's story.

Since opening its doors on the anniversary of D-Day on June 6, 2000, the National WWII Museum has enjoyed considerable success with over 706,664 visitors in 2017 and has contributed significantly to New Orleans's cultural scene. The Museum has generated about $ 132 million in annual economic impact for the state of Louisiana and has totaled more than $ 1.38 billion in direct and indirect impact since 2000.

1. US Freedom Pavilion: The Boeing Center, 2013. Photo: From the collection of the National WWII Museum.
2. Campaigns of the Courage Pavilion, 2015. Photo: From the collection of the National WWII Museum.
3. Campus site plan. The Louisiana Memorial Pavilion was the National WWII Museum's first building (2000), and the last will be the Liberation Pavilion (scheduled for completion in 2020). Photo: Voorsanger Mathes LLC.
4. Rendering of the »Bollinger Canopy of Peace«, 2018. Photo: Voorsanger Mathies LLC.

pp. 116, 117
5. Detail of the »Battle of the Bulge« exhibition in the campaigns of Courage Pavilion, 2015. Photo: From the collection of the National WWII Museum.
6. Detail from »The Arsenal of Democracy« exhibition, 2017 in the Louisiana Memorial Pavilion. From the collection of the National WWII Museum.
7. US Freedom Pavilion: The Boeing Center, 2013, atrium showing suspended American aircraft such as a B-25 Mitchell and TBM Avenger. Photo: From the collection of the National WWII Museum.

LIBERATION PAVILION
CAMPAIGNS PAVILION
LAND, SEA AND AIR PAVILION
PARADE GROUND & LANDSCAPE OF WAR
CENTRAL PLANT
SPECIAL EXHIBITION & COLLECTION PAVILION
STAGE DOOR CANTEEN & EXECUTIVE OFFICES
THEATER PAVILION
LOUISIANA PAVILION

WE'RE ALL IN IT
MUST WIN!
TRAINING EXERCISES
SEE WHAT RECRUITS WOULD HAVE LEARNED
TRAINING FOR LAND
AMPHIBIOUS TRAINING
TRAINING FOR SEA

U.S. NAVY

**Royal Air Force Museum, Colindale, London, England. Addition and master plan, 2018**
Nex-Architecture

2018 marked the centennial of the Royal Air Force/RAF. Its museum at the former airfield at Colindale, formerly Hendon in north London, opened in 1972. Expansions were made in 1978 and 1983, with the airfield actually closing 1987. Of the early buildings there the Grahame-White aircraft factory structure from the early twentieth century remains along with several RAF buildings. The museum itself occupies five exhibition hangars – halls with over 100 aircraft, more than tripling the number of airframes when it first opened. With its collection ever growing, the museum established facilities at Cosford (see p. 54). Together, each of these museum locations has an annual attendance of some 350,000. With the approaching centenary, and the need to coordinate expansion at the London site on its more than 19 acres (7.7 ha), the museum held a design competition that was won in 2014 by Nex-Architecture and Agence Ter. Their principals Alan Dempsey and Olivier Philippe provided a master plan for its future; including detailed design for landscape and num-ber of buildings. This is to be phased over five years.

Their plan eliminated the car park at the center of the complex, thereby giving visitors an idea of what the original airfield was like in this open green space. As part of this, the existing aluminum-skinned Hangar 1, was cleaned and remodeled as the main entrance for the entire site. The remodeled entrance building has within it a café, museum shop, and corporate event space. These facilities could also be used by outside groups without necessarily wanting to see the entire museum complex. This would encourage community engagement as well. The façade renovation provides a new 131 feet (40 m) long entry on the north elevation. Inside the building, previously built walls were demolished to create open spaces and services. Visitors will see RAF centenary exhibitions there created by Kossmann.dejong + Met Studio before proceeding to the massive Short Sunderland flying boat in this 40 feet (12.2 m) high space which signals their exit to other buildings and exhibits on the site. This large central volume of the building has an acoustic lining and also extruded aluminum fins as a design element that links the building, visually, to aircraft on display throughout the complex. The building took one year to complete, 2017/18.

Finally, Building 52, the former derelict 1930s brick and steel officer's mess from the base, was converted into a new 170 seat restaurant along with additional space within for two private event rooms. The restaurant interiors have ash paneling and oak flooring. The renovated Hangar 1, now the visitor center, is a 55,972 square feet (5,200 sq. m) building whereas the restaurant building is 6,889 square feet (640 sq. m). The project was supported by the Heritage Lottery Fund and the total budget was £ 9 Million.

1. Overall view from the airfield green at night, showing Short Sunderland. Photo: © Alan Williams, courtesy Nex.
2. Detail of the campus master plan, showing plan for the renovated Hangar 1. Photo: courtesy Nex.
3. Hangar 1 rendered in a special event configuration. Photo: courtesy Nex.

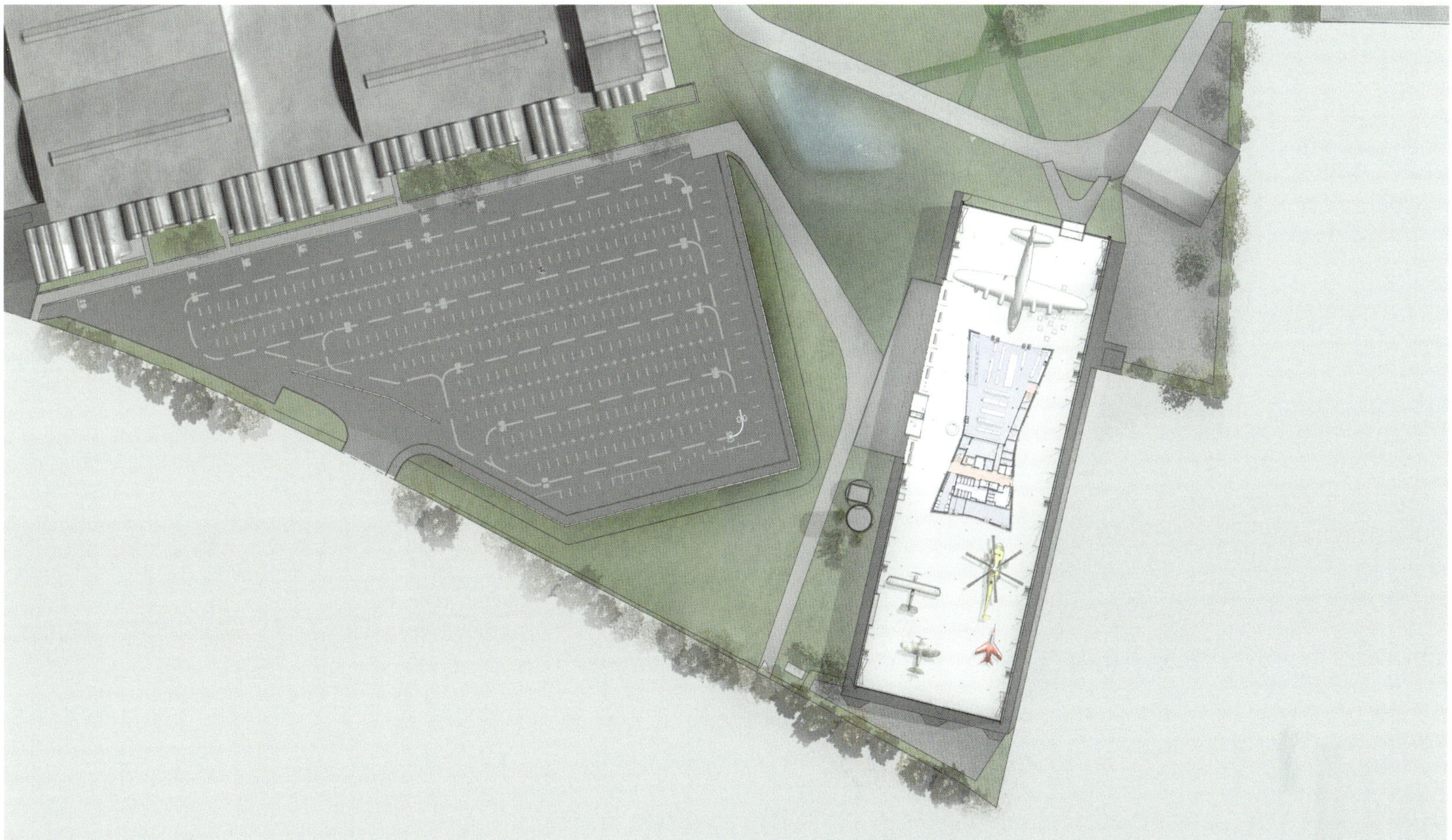

4, 5. Hangar 1 interiors in 2018. Photos: © Alan Williams, courtesy Nex.

**National Museum of the U.S. Army, Fort Belvoir, Virginia, USA, 2017–18, 2020**
Skidmore, Owings & Merrill

The National Museum of the U.S. Army project began in 2008, when international architecture firm Skidmore, Owings & Merrill was awarded the commission. SOM Design Partner Roger Duffy is leading the design of the project. Christopher Chadbourne & Associates was initially chosen as the exhibit designer, but was replaced after the firm closed. Eisterhold was selected in 2012 as the new exhibition designer, basing the design on Chadbourne's preliminary construction documents. The project is a public-private partnership with the United States Army as well as the Army Museum Foundation, established in 2000 as part of the Army Museum Enterprise. The latter is a consortium of U.S. Army museums across the United States.

SOM planned the museum to accommodate 500,000 to 750,000 visitors each year, an estimate that is comparable to the attendance of other such service museums in suburban Washington, D.C., most notably the Marine Corps Museum (see p. 44). Ground breaking took place in 2016 and the museum is slated to open to the public in 2020. Funded by the Army Museum Foundation, the 185,000 square feet (17,187 sq. m) museum is estimated to cost is $ 250 million. The 80 acres (32.38 ha) site includes a memorial garden, parade ground for ceremonies, and a 200-seat amphitheater, along with a large area for parking and tour buses. The museum is expected to accommodate some of the 16,000 paintings from the Army's art collection within their displays as well as 30,000 artifacts and documents. The museum building will also have visitor service facilities and a café and museum store.

The five-story, steel-clad building will contain artifacts, immersive experiences, and interactive displays that focus on individual soldier stories, as well as an education space that concentrates on STEM (Science, Technology, Engineering and Math) activities. As with its London counterpart (see p. 104), there will be a large gallery of 9,000 square feet (836 sq. m) on the Army and society. SOM's design features a series of massing volumes that are intended to be acropolis-like, breaking up the overall size of the large structure. The lobby will have a black granite donor wall with gold leaf text inscribed as well as a like-designed campaign wall. The lobby ceiling will contain campaign ribbons related to the Army's service throughout the centuries back to the American Revolution. As with many other buildings of this type, large scale artifacts such as tanks were situated within the structure before it was closed. The museum is intended to commemorate the more than 30 million American men and women who have served in the U.S. Army. The National Museum of the U.S. Army at Fort Belvoir will be the high profile public face of the Army, whereas the U.S. Army Heritage & Education Center at Carlisle Barracks in Pennsylvania, despite having extensive gallery exhibits and educational programs, will remain the location of the Army's main research and history facility, in tandem with the nearby U.S. Army War College.

1. Rendering of overall view.
2. Plan and partial section.
Photos: © Skidmore, Owings & Merrill.

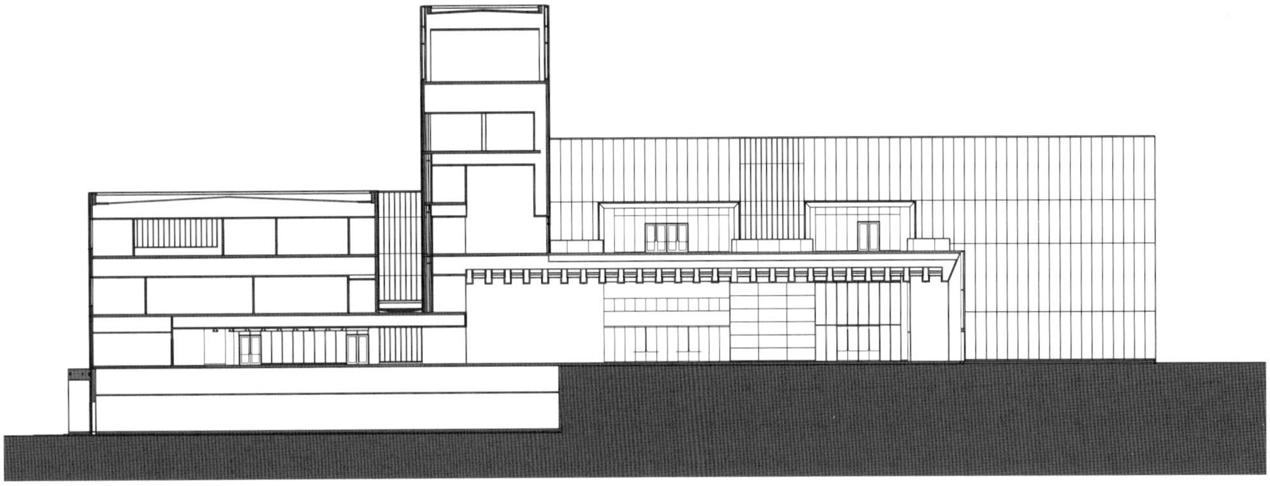

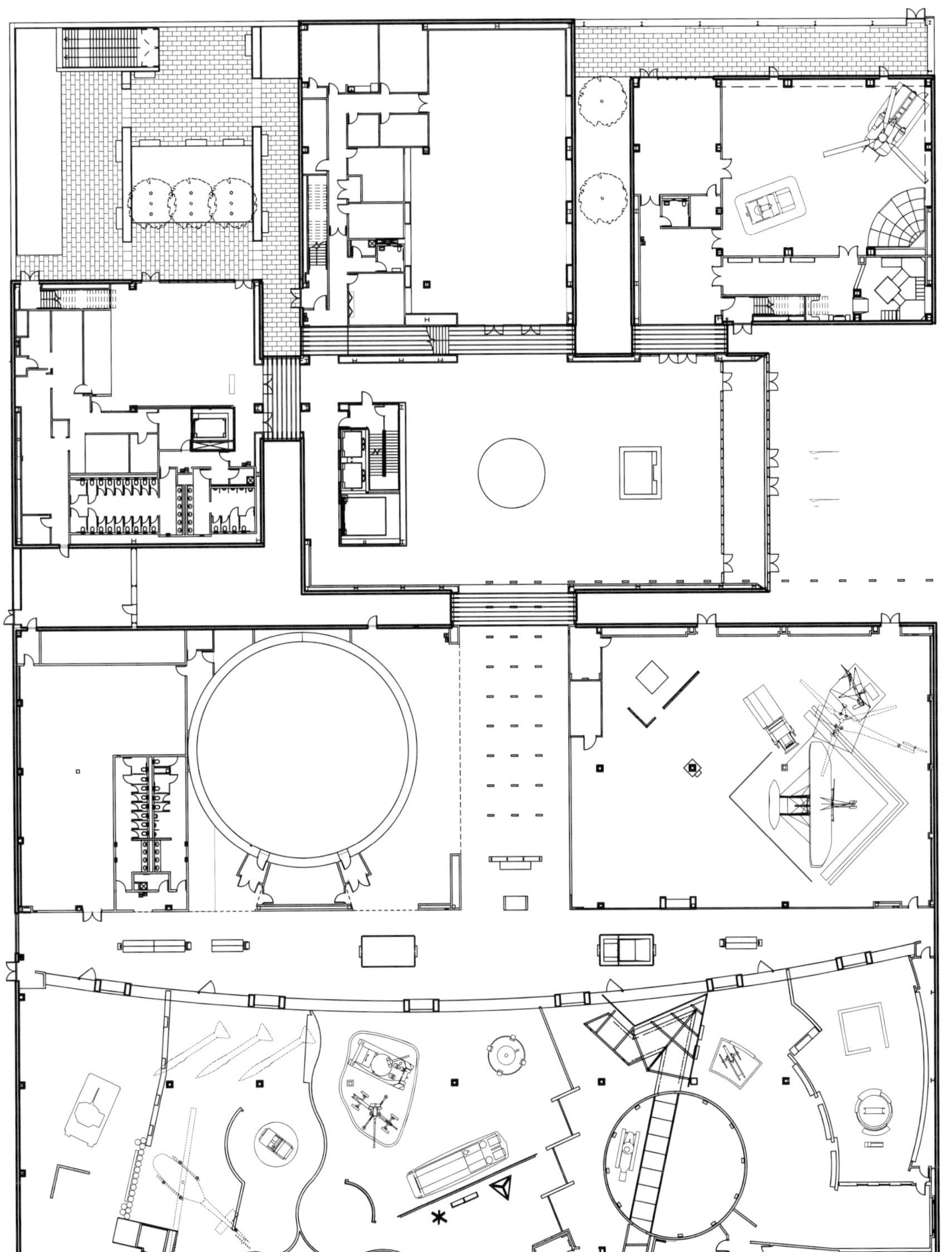

VALOR
GALLANTRY
INTREPIDITY

3,4. Renderings of the Medal of Honor Garden and the museum lobby. Photos: © Skidmore, Owings & Merrill.

## Selected sources

There are numerous websites available regarding buildings pictured and discussed within this book. The best available ones are often those for the architects and exhibition designers as well as the museums themselves. Some of those museums have also been published and reviewed in a variety of architectural periodicals, and researchers may find hard copies of those within various libraries as well as in online editions. Internet urls are not listed here because they sometimes change over time. The reader is encouraged to search relevant keywords related to those individual museums and designers. In addition to that online searching, this selection of books and journal articles, many on war memorials but some also referencing museum discussion within, may also be useful. Most were located within research libraries within my own city at the Pritzker Military Museum & Library, as well as the Ryerson and Burnham Libraries of the Art Institute of Chicago.


*Arup Associates. Selected and Current Works.* Mulgrave, Victoria, Australia, 1994.

Nils Ballhausen, »Militär-Museum«, *Bauwelt*, 106/8 (2015), pp. 26–33.

Teresa Bergman, *Exhibiting Patriotism*. Walnut Creek, California, 2013.

Mark Blackburn, *Interpreting American Military History at Museums and Historic Sites*. London, 2016.

Alan Borg, *War Memorials from Antiquity to the Present.* London, 1991.

»Breaking the Symmetry: Military History Museum, Dresden«, *Architecture+Design*, 29/6 (June 2012), pp. 52–57.

Ryan Coonerty, *Etched in Stone: Enduring Words from our Nation's Monuments*. Washington, D.C., 2007.

»Daniel Libeskind: The Imperial War Museum North, Manchester, U.K.«, *A+U*, 385 (October 2002), pp. 14–23.

David Dillion, introduction, *Fentress Bradburn Architects. Museums and Theaters*. New York, 2003.

Barrie Evans, »Concrete in Flight«, *Architects' Journal*, 206/17 (1997), pp. 51–54.

»Feilden Clegg Bradbury Architects: National Cold War Exhibition, RAF Museum, Cosford«, *A+U*, 664 (June 2007), pp. 100–103.

Helmut and Alison Gernsheim, *L.J.M Daguerre. The History of the Diorama and the Daguerreotype*. New York, 1968.

Alastair Gordon, *Bartholomew Voorsanger. Unfolded: How Architecture Saved My Life*. New York, 2017.

Rob Gregory, »Chill in the Air«, *Architectural Review*, 221/1320 (February 2007), pp. 32–33.

Nicholas Hirsch and Wolfgang Lorch, »Precarious Landscape: Hinzert Museum and Document Centre«, *AA Files*, 52 (July 2005), pp. 2–7.

Benjamin J. Hruska, *Interpreting Naval History at Museums and Historic Sites*. London, 2016.

Arata Isozaki, »Jianchuan Museum Complex – Japanese Army Museum, Chengdu, China, Design: 2004–05, Construction: 2006– «, *GA Document*, 91 (2006), pp. 74–79.

Mike Jones, »Foster Solves the Big Span Problem in Precast Concrete«, *Architects' Journal*, 198/2 (1993), pp. 25–27.

Diane Lees interview, »Lasting Legacies«, *Apollo*, 180/622 (July 2014), pp. 25–26.

Diana Lind, »The Battle for History«, *Architectural Record*, 205/7 (July 2017), p. 78.

James N. Mayo, *War Memorials as Political Landscape: The American Experience and Beyond*. New York, 1988.

Rowan Moore, »Military History Museum Review«, *The Guardian* (October 23, 2011).

Raymond Moriyama, *In Search of a Soul. Designing and Realizing the New Canadian War Museum*. Toronto, 2006.

»Museumscenter Bla'vand, Varde, Denmark, 2011«, *A+U* 548 (May 2016), pp. 138–143.

Ulrike Nicholson, »National Military Museum in Soesterberg«, *Architektur, Innenarchitektur, Technischer Ausbau*, 3 (2016), pp. 122–127.

Sheperd Paine, *How to Build Dioramas*. Milwaukee, 1980.

G. Kurt Piehler, *Remembering War the American Way.* Washington, D.C., 1995.

Mark Quinlan, *British War Memorials.* Hereford, England, 2005.

Steve Rajtar, *War Monuments, Museums and Library Collections of 20th Century Conflicts: A Directory of United States Sites.* Jefferson, North Carolina, 2010.

Ruth Slavid, »Unfolding a Narrative«, *The Architects Journal* 204, no. 6 (August 15, 1996), pp. 18–19.

Alastair Soooke, »The New-Look Imperial War Museum: Affecting and Poignant«, *The Telegraph* (July 16, 2014),

Suzanne Stephens, »Smithgroup: Normandy American Cemetery Visitor Center«, *Architectural Record*,196 (March 2008), pp. 112–117.

James B. Sweeney, *A Pictorial Guide to the Military Museums, Forts and Historic Sites of the United States.* New York, 1981.

Bryce D. Thompson, *U.S. Military Museums, Historic Sites & Exhibits*. Falls Church, Virginia, 1989.

Peter Thwaites, *Presenting Arms: Museum Representation of British Military History, 1660–1900.* London, 1996.

Patricia Anne Vertinsky and Sherry McKay, eds., *Disciplining Bodies in the Gymnasium: Memory, Monument, Modernism*. London, 2004.

Ian Volner, »Robert Stern's Museum of the American Revolution«, *Architect*, 106/6 (June 2017), pp. 103–110.

Volker Welter, »Kriegsmachinen und Flughafen-Romantik. Das American Air Museum in Duxford«, *Bauwelt*, 88/35 (1997), pp. 1924–1927.

»Winglike Canopy Will Shelter Air Force Museum«, *Progressive Architecture*, 45 (December 1964), pp. 182–184.

Herbert Wright, »Museum of the Second World War Kwadrat«, *Blueprint*, 352 (May/June 2017), pp. 50–64.

John Zukowsky, »Monumental American Obelisks: Centennial Vistas«, *The Art Bulletin*, 58/4 (December 1976), pp. 574–581.

## Acknowledgments

I began thinking about a book such as this when I was Chief Curator at the Intrepid Sea, Air & Space Museum 2005–09 as well as Interim Director of the Pritzker Military Museum and Library in 2010. As I familiarized myself with military museums at that time, I realized that a number had gone well beyond the mom-and-pop, somewhat amateurish operations that typified stereotypes of that sort of museum. This was true not only in their operations but also in their architecture and exhibition design. After mostly retiring from the museum world in 2012, a book on those great buildings and installations became more than a back-burner project as I attempted to find grant support and a publisher. In working on those possibilities on and off for five years, I was fortunate to reconnect with Capt. Dave Truitt. He is a Chicagoan who has been an integral part of museums and exhibits for decades, including ones with important military artifacts such as the *U-505* installation at the Museum of Science and Industry and the Douglas Dauntless SBD dive bomber displayed at Chicago's Midway International Airport. It was Dave who heartily endorsed and supported my idea in 2018 to honor those who served and sacrificed with this book on newer military museums, and I am very thankful for his support. With that secured, I approached several publishers. Axel Menges and Dorothea Duwe of Edition Axel Menges, stepped up with an offer to produce this volume as part of their surveys on various topics in architecture and design. Their work on this final product is, as always, admirable.

Although I had developed something of a short list of buildings for inclusion over the past few years, I dedicated a good portion of my time in 2018 to research and compile the imagery for this book. What can be found inside this volume, in terms of information as well as imagery, is the result of active cooperation with a wide variety of architects, designers, photographers, and museums, all of whom deserve my sincere gratitude. Fellow author Ron Werneth introduced me to his friend Ikuo »Ike« Shimizu. Ike was instrumental in securing the cooperation of the Bansei Peace Museum and Yamato Museum. This is certainly something that I would not have been able to do myself, so he deserves my particular thanks here.

Colleagues who are historians and researchers, as well as those in museums, and who happily assisted me include: Ayumi Kido for the Bansei Peace Museum of the city government of Minamisatsuma; David Kenyon, Peronel Craddock, Gemma Briggs and Liz McCaffry Payne at Bletchley Park; Marie-Louise Deruaz, Avra Gibbs-Lamey, Kathryn Lyons, and Susan Ross of the Canadian War Museum; Paul Herbert and Dave Blake of the First Division Museum; Angela Hoover of the Chicago History Museum; Suzanne Bardgett of the Imperial War Museum; Susan Marenoff-Zausner, Mike Onysko, and Erin Devaney of the Intrepid Sea, Air & Space Museum; Nathalie Worthington and Mike Bechthold of Juno Beach Centre; Claire Lawrence of the Kitsap Conference Center; Christoph Lehmann of the Militärhistorisches Museum der Bundeswehr; Michael C. Quinn of the Museum of the American Revolution; Quintrel Brown of the National Museum of the American Sailor; Ken LaRock of the National Museum of the United States Air Force; Mike Vietti of the National World War I Museum and Memorial; Tessa Jagger at the National World War II Museum; Elissa Lines of the Pacific Aviation Museum at Pearl Harbor; Megan Williams and Rachel Kosmal of the Pritzker Military Museum & Library; Lindy Dosher and Megan Churchwell of the Puget Sound Navy Museum; Michela Johnson of the RAF Museum; and Paul Dolan and Roz Skellorn of the Tank Museum UK. I am grateful to all my museum colleagues who helped supply me with information as well as photos.

As with museum employees, the staff of architects, exhibition designers, and contractors also went above and beyond in their assistance, and I thank them very much for their efforts. They include: Ellen Sandor and Janine Fron of ARTN; Julianne McAtarsney of BDP; Michele Camacho of Chamberlain Architect Services; Noel Abbott of Epstein; Jason Knowles of Fentress Architects; Patrick Gallagher, Gretchen Coss, Carl Rhodes and Jenna Goff of Gallagher & Associates; Katy Harris and Gayle Mault of Foster + Partners; Matt Larson of Goettsch Partners; Janie Price of Kennedy O'Callaghan Architects; Jasmin Blomme of Felix Claus Dick Van Wageningen Architekten; Todd Imming of the Korte Co.; Hannah Geerdink of Kossmann.dejong; Pawel Sikora of Archiktoniczne Studio Kwadrat; Martina Dolejsova of Studio Libeskind; Breana Coco and A.J. Goehe of Luci Creative; Audra Waterbury of Maltbie; Glenn Mason Architect; Nicole Liao and Chris Yen of Moriyama and Teshima; Sophie Arvidsson of Nex; J.D. McKibben of Perkins+Will; Tim Burton of SH Structures; Roger Duffy and Frank Mahan with Emma Bird, and Nickolas Massar of Skidmore, Owings & Merrill; Gillian Mitchell at the Steel Association; Peter Morris Dixon and Alexander P. Lamis at Robert A.M. Stern Architects; Brad Nederhoff of Verner Johnson, Inc.; Paul Kraemer at Vinci Hamp Architects; Bart Voorsanger and the head of his archives Victoria Young at the University of St. Thomas in Minnesota; Stacey Linh of Warehaus; architect Sara Ebrahem in Egypt; and engineer Ahmed Said Hassan in Saudi Arabia; and Maureen Joyce of Midway International Airport.

Photographers and their staff certainly rounded out all the colleagues who actively assisted in making their imagery available, particularly at hi-resolution, and I very much thank them: Mark Ballogg of Ballogg Photography; Benjamin Benschneider; Jan Bitter of Bitter Bredt; Len Grant; Allan Crow of Hufton and Crow; Roland Halbe and Steffi Steimle; Matt Kosterman; Guillaume Murat; Shaun Armstrong of MUBSTA; Melissa LeBoeuf and Vicky Saperstein of OTTO; Christian Richters; and Frederick Granger of Van Rhijn Aerial Photography.

If I have missed anyone who has participated with me in this publishing journey, I apologize. As I close this list I must thank Milli my wife for all the support she has always given me in projects such as these. And for all those who have served and will serve their countries, and who are chronicled in museums such as those within this volume, I dedicate this book to you.

John Zukowsky, Chicago

John Zukowsky is an architectural and design historian with more than four decades of museum experience. He has an earned doctorate from Binghamton University and has been the recipient of awards and honors from the American Institute of Architects, the Society of Architectural Historians, and the republics of Austria and France. While curator of architecture for The Art Institute of Chicago (1978–2004), he organized a number of award-winning exhibitions accompanied by major books. After that, he held executive positions within museums in Ohio, Chicago and New York. The last was as Chief Curator and then Interim Vice President for Exhibitions and Interpretation, at the Intrepid Sea, Air & Space Museum (2005–09 and 2011/12 respectively). There, he spearheaded the team on the reinstallation and exhibition redesign for that National Historic Landmark as well as the temporary installation of the Space Shuttle *Enterprise*. Since then he has authored several books about architecture and design, including *Why on Earth Would Anyone Build That. Modern Architecture Explained* (2015), *Building Chicago: The Architectural Masterworks* (2016), and *Architecture Inside – Out: Understanding How Buildings Work* (2018).